PARLIAMENTARY PROCEDURE AT A GLANCE

Group Leadership Manual for
Chairmanship and Floor Leadership

BY

O. GARFIELD JONES

PROFESSOR OF POLITICAL SCIENCE IN THE
UNIVERSITY OF TOLEDO

New Enlarged and Revised Edition

FOREWORD BY

LEHR FESS

FORMER PARLIAMENTARIAN
UNITED STATES HOUSE OF REPRESENTATIVES

PENGUIN BOOKS

PENGUIN BOOKS
Published by the Penguin Group
Viking Penguin, a division of Penguin Books USA Inc., 375 Hudson Street,
New York, New York 10014, U.S.A.
Penguin Books Ltd, 27 Wrights Lane, London W8 5TZ, England
Penguin Books Australia Ltd, Ringwood, Victoria, Australia
Penguin Books Canada Ltd, 2801 John Street, Markham, Ontario, Canada L3R 1B4
Penguin Books (N.Z.) Ltd, 182–190 Wairau Road, Auckland 10, New Zealand

Penguin Books Ltd, Registered Offices:
Harmondsworth, Middlesex, England

Revised edition published by Hawthorn/Dutton 1971
Published in Penguin Books 1990

10 9 8 7 6 5 4 3 2

Library of Congress Catalog Card Number: 77–161641 (Dutton)

ISBN 0 14 01.5328 4

Printed in the United States of America

TO MY WIFE
NELLIE NIXON JONES

Preface

With one exception this manual contains all the rules in common use governing the discussion and action of groups other than legislative bodies in the United States. The technical rules of procedure used in legislatures are impractical for the ordinary civilian group both because they are quite complicated in order to meet the needs of a large body with a tremendous volume of business and because no two legislatures have exactly the same rules. For instance, on the motion "to table" one set of rules applies in the United States House of Representatives, a different set of rules applies in the Ohio Legislature, and still another set applies in the Legislature of Indiana.

General Henry M. Robert performed a truly great service for the American people when in 1876 he simplified the rules of procedure of the U. S. House of Representatives so as to adapt them to the use of ordinary societies and got this "adaptation" accepted generally throughout the United States as the "standard rules of order" for group meetings.

This Manual neither changes nor supersedes General Robert's splendid "Rules of Order" (except for a minor detail noted below).

This Manual, Parliamentary Procedure at a Glance, is primarily a pedagogical contribution that enables any ordinary person to use Robert's "Rules" effectively without committing the rules to memory.

The one modification of Robert's "Rules" to be found in Parliamentary Procedure at a Glance is that the motion "to reconsider and have entered on the minutes for action at the next meeting" is not included in my manual, although the regular motion "to Reconsider" is in this manual (page 19). According to Robert's "Rules" the motion **to reconsider and have entered on the minutes for action at the next meeting** takes precedence over the regular motion **"to reconsider"** and thus enables two obstreperous members to prevent final action on any motion at one meeting no matter how important.

General Robert recognized this difficulty but suggested that this paralysis of action by two members may be overcome by having the club vote to have a special meeting next day at which time this **"special"** motion to reconsider may be voted down and the main motion to which it applied be put into effect. But how many organizations are in a position to call a special meeting next day to remove the barrier to final action set up by two contrary members who have paralyzed immediate action by the assembly on a matter of urgent importance to which these two contrary members happen to be opposed? It is my contention that there is less probability of abuse of the regular motion "**to reconsider**" by the majority than there is probability of the abuse of the motion "**to reconsider and have entered on the minutes for action at the next meeting**" by any two members of the assembly.

These lessons for teaching parliamentary procedure and group leadership are the product of fourteen years experience in teaching some three thousand students. Messrs. Virgil Sheppard, J. Otis Garber, H. T. Shenefield, Orville R. Altman, Donovan F. Emch, and Charles F. Carson have contributed to the evolution of this teaching technique while conducting classes by this system. Mr. Lehr Fess, sometime Parliamentarian of the United States House of Representatives, has contributed much in the way of advice as to technical procedure both as teacher of Congressional Procedure in my department one year and as personal consultant on difficult points.

Mr. Brenton W. Stevenson read the entire proof, saved me from many errors and added much to the general form and appearance of the pages.

Dr. Raymond L. Carter gave many suggestions and criticisms that materially improved the technical pedagogy of the lessons. I am especially indebted to students in my classes on "teaching group leadership" whose suggestions contributed much to the adaptation of this technique to public school use.

Perhaps I am most indebted to those students who have so demonstrated the value of this group leadership technique in college, and later, as to provide the chief inspiration for the working out of these manuals.

O. G. J.

FOREWORD

Fundamentally all law is based on custom. Like the common law, parliamentary law is largely based upon the customary practices regulating procedure in group action as developed throughout the centuries. While the fundamental rules are applicable to all group action, a wide difference in detail must necessarily exist when the rules are applied to different groups. For example, the rules of the House of Representatives which afford the basis of most texts on parliamentary law in this country must meet the needs of a body of over four hundred persons meeting daily for months with a great volume of business. Therefore, these rules can not be used in detail by a convention or smaller groups of citizens organized for more or less informal action and convening intermittently.

Technical procedure should be discouraged in legislative bodies and to a greater degree in ordinary parliamentary groups. Rules should be applied and interpreted so as to permit a majority to accomplish its ultimate purpose within a reasonable period of time but only after allowing the minority reasonable opportunity to express its views on the question at issue.

The work of Dr. Jones is unique in its simplicity. The variations from the rules laid down by other texts which he suggests should result in simplifying procedure and should aid in the avoidance of technical complications which are often so irksome to the layman and discourage his interest in parliamentary law. Dr. Jones is making a substantial contribution toward a more effective democracy by his simple application of common sense to procedure in group action.

Lehr Fess

INTRODUCTION

Leadership

The effective individual functions through groups, many groups. It is the group that gives him weight in every field of endeavor. Therefore, the effective individual must be effective in groups, that is, he must be a group leader—not necessarily the chairman of the group, but at least the leader of some activity or policy of the group.

Group leadership is an art that anyone can learn, first by learning the rules for group discussion and action called parliamentary procedure, second by practice in the art of leadership. This Group Leadership Manual is designed to provide the rules of procedure for a chairman or a member just as they are needed and without preliminary study. It also provides parliamentary phrases which facilitate practice in the art, the strategy, of group leadership.

The Rules of Parliamentary Procedure are the Basis of Constitutional Government

Democratic government is based abolutely upon the principle of majority rule. But majority rule requires that the minority abide by the will of the majority. And the willingness of the minority to abide by the will of the majority is, in turn, based upon the willingness of the majority **to permit the minority to "have their say"** before final action is taken. The cry of Themistocles to Eurybiades was "Strike, but hear me!"

As has been said so frequently, the chief purpose of parliamentary procedure is to protect the rights of the minority. The majority can usually take care of itself. In a government controlled by public opinion, which we call a democracy, accepted rules of parliamentary procedure are not only of the highest importance for legislatures, they are the foundation of freedom in every meeting, large or small, throughout the nation.

Good citizenship is a habit of dealing with one's fellow citizens. It is the habit of giving one's best thoughts and efforts for the general welfare but at the same time being willing to consider the thoughts and efforts of others, and, if need be, compromising with or submitting to the thoughts and efforts of the majority of one's fellow citizens. This habit of participation in, compromising with, and submission to the will of the majority may be acquired only as other habits are acquired; by practice, and then more practice.

This Group Leadership Manual is designed to facilitate the development of this type of good citizenship conduct by making it possible for all the groups in the country, be they highly educated or not, to conduct their meetings according to the accepted rules of parliamentary procedure that have been worked out by a thousand years of English and American experience in self-government through deliberative assemblies.

Effective Groups

For a group to be of maximum effectiveness it must have competent leadership and also a high degree of competence among its members. Among other things this implies that the members know how to deliberate and how to crystallize these deliberations into group action. This also implies that the chairman knows how to inspire and direct group discussion and how to facilitate the crystallizing of this discussion into specific group action.

CHAIRMANSHIP

A good chairman is one who inspires confidence by his assurance, and who keeps the assembly informed at all times as to what is before them for consideration and vote. However, no chairman can inspire confidence and maintain the dignity of the assembly when he is making one erroneous decision after another. Correctness is a matter of fact, not a matter of conceit.

This Group Leadership Manual provides instantaneously the facts which enable a competent citizen to be correct in his decisions as chairman or correct in his conduct as an active member of the assembly.

Dignity and leadership are personal qualities that are dependent in part only on being correct. But a citizen with an average amount of personality may, by practice, develop dignity and leadership ability if he is correct in his conduct in the group.

Just as the dictionary enables any literate person to spell correctly when writing a letter, just so does this manual enable any citizen to function in a civic, business, educational or other discussion group either as a chairman or as an active member.

Group discussion and group action, like group games, require rules for their operation. The rules for group discussion and group action are commonly called "parliamentary procedure" because they were first worked out into a complete scheme by a thousand years of English and American legislative experience.

However, all the elaborate and detailed rules used by a state or national legislature are not necessary for the conduct of business in a small club or group. All the technical knowledge and experience needed when operating an aeroplane are not needed when operating a motorcycle, less still when operating a tricycle.

It is a waste of time for the ordinary citizen to attempt to master all the formal rules of procedure for conducting business in a group because the detailed rules are too numerous for the human mind to retain and use with facility just as learning to spell all the words in the dictionary is not worth while unless one is contesting for the spelling championship of the United States. For most of us it is sufficient to have the dictionary handy so that we can spell correctly the words we actually use from day to day. The fact is that by the quick use of a dictionary the average man can readily out-spell the expert speller who does not have the use of a dictionary.

In similar manner the average citizen may by the use of this manual more readily and correctly decide points of parliamentary procedure than can the expert parliamentarian who has no such reference manual to use. This is so because the general philosophy of procedure which the expert parliamentarian does know may not always suffice to solve certain technical points that are more arbitrary than philosophical just as the general rules of spelling do not always suffice in determining the spelling of proper names for the simple reason that the spelling of proper names is frequently determined by the arbitrary will of the owner of the name rather than by the general rules of spelling. In short, the average citizen needs to know enough parliamentary procedure to fill satisfactorily the group position in which he finds himself from time to time. To know less is to seriously reduce his efficiency. To know more requires, as a rule, more time than he can devote to the subject.

This Group Leadership Manual has been devised to fill this specific need of the busy citizen. An adult of superior ability can use this manual without any previous study other than to learn the sequence of motions. This sequence must be learned in order that the user of the manual may turn to any motion on the instant. This sequence is not according to alphabetical order. On the contrary, the sequence of motions in this manual is their sequence in rank or precedence. That is to say, any motion indexed on the left hand side takes precedence of those on the right hand side, and any motion on either side takes precedence over the motions that are below it on that side (with certain indicated exceptions). Or, stated conversely, any motion indexed on the right hand side yields to any motion indexed on the left side, and any motion below yields to any motion indexed above it on the same side. Variations from this general rule are clearly indicated under each motion involved in the variation.

CLASSIFICATION AND PRECEDENCE
OF MOTIONS

The main motion (page 18) is the main idea or resolution that the assembly is working on, such as, "I move that we have a picnic Friday afternoon." You can have only one such main idea before the assembly at any one time. To have two main but distinct ideas before the assembly at one time would cause endless confusion both in the discussion and in the voting. Therefore, the main motion has the lowest rank or "precedence" of all the motions because a main motion can be moved only when there is nothing else before the assembly.

Now, when a main motion, such as "to have a picnic Friday afternoon" is before the assembly, any of the motions above it (pages 1 to 17) may be moved. That is to say, any member of the assembly may move to "amend the motion by adding the words 'in Sunset Park'," or move "to refer this picnic idea to the entertainment committee," or move "to postpone consideration of this 'picnic' motion until tomorrow," or move "to close debate on this 'picnic' motion," or move "to lay this 'picnic' motion on the table," (that is lay it aside for the present), or "rise for information" and ask if there is to be no school Friday afternoon, or move "to adjourn."

All of these motions take **precedence** over the main motion because they apply to the main motion or, as in the case of the motion to adjourn, they are of such immediate importance to the assembly that they must be voted on at once regardless of what else is before the assembly.

The motion to adjourn is called a "privileged motion" because it is of such importance to the assembly that it must be acted on at once. Suppose the furnace was filling the room with smoke so rapidly that the members of the assembly could hardly breathe. Obviously it would be absurd to remain in the smoke-filled room to continue the discussion on "the picnic." Some member should move to **adjourn**. The chairman would put this to a vote, and if the majority were in favor of adjournment the Chair would declare the assembly adjourned regardless of any other motions that might be before the assembly.

"To rise" to a point of order, or for information, is called an incidental motion, because while it does not apply to the main motion "to have a picnic" it is **incidental to it**. Thus the person who "rose for information" and asked "Is there to be no school Friday afternoon?" wanted to know the answer to this question before he voted on the motion to have a picnic. If there was to be no school, then he was in favor of the picnic, but if there **was to be** school he was not in favor of having the picnic. A person might rise to a point of order and then tell the Chair that there was too much noise in the room.

This "incidental" motion has precedence over the main motion because the member wants his question answered before the vote is taken on the "motion to have a picnic Friday afternoon" or wants the assembly to be more quiet so he can hear the discussion.

Thus it is easy to see why the motion "to adjourn" and "rising to a point of order" or "for information" are permitted to interrupt other business and must be acted on at once.

The motions (12 to 17) that apply to the main motion and take precedence over it are called subsidiary motions because they are "subsidiary to the main motion." They have no purpose in themselves. Their only purpose is to affect the main motion. Thus the purpose of the motion to amend is to change the main motion; the motion to refer, the motion to postpone consideration, and the motion to table all serve to dispose of the main motion temporarily, while the motion to close debate, if passed by a two-thirds vote, cuts off any further discussion.

Thus we have the four classes of motions: privileged (pages 1 to 4), incidental (pages 5 to 11), subsidiary (pages 12 to 17), and main (page 18). These motions are arranged in the manual according to their rank or precedence, the one of lowest rank at the bottom (page 18) and the one of the highest rank at the top (page 1). And this ranking is absolute (with a few exceptions to be explained later) so that any motion can be moved when a motion below it in precedence is before the assembly. Conversely, no motion can be moved if a motion above it in precedence is before the assembly. Thus if someone moved that we have a picnic Friday afternoon, and someone else moved that this motion "be referred to the entertainment committee," then the motion to "amend the main motion by adding the words 'Sunset Park'" would be "out of order" because the motion to refer does not yield to the motion to amend, or, conversely the motion to amend does not take precedence over the motion to refer.

Of course, if the motion to refer is voted down, then the motion to amend may be used because then the motion to refer is no longer before the assembly; it has been disposed of by a negative vote.

On the other hand it is possible to have seven motions before the assembly at one time provided they are made in the right sequence; that is, if a main motion was moved, then an amendment to that motion, then the motion to refer, then the motion to postpone consideration until tomorrow, then the motion to close debate, then the motion to lay on the table, then a point of order was raised, and finally it was moved to adjourn. (The point of order would be decided by the Chair as soon as it was raised, consequently, it would not be pending when the motion to adjourn was moved.)

XIV

When seven persons desire **recognition** in rapid succession to make different motions the thing to do is to ignore some of them until some of the motions already before the assembly are decided by vote. The chairman has other responsibilities besides recognizing persons who desire to exhibit their technical knowledge of parliamentary procedure, and one of these other responsibilities is to keep things as simple as possible for the assembly.

However, these seven motions could be moved in this sequence and in such rapid succession that all seven would be pending at one time in strict conformity to the rules of order, but it would be nothing but a "stunt"; it would not serve any useful purpose except to illustrate the order of precedence of these seven motions and demonstrate the high privilege of the motion to adjourn in that it must be voted on at once even though these other six motions are all pending before the assembly.

Note:—If the assembly voted "No" on each of these motions in turn, then each would have to be voted upon, but in reverse order. That is, the vote would be first on the motion to adjourn. As stated above the point of order would have been decided by the Chair as soon as it was raised; consequently, no vote would be required on the point of order, or on any point of information. The second vote would be on the motion to table, the third vote would be on the motion to close debate and the fourth would be on the motion to postpone till the next meeting. However, if the motion to close debate was defeated by a negative vote, then the chairman would be compelled to announce **"The noes have it by more than a one-third vote and the motion to close debate is lost. Is there any discussion on the motion to postpone consideration till the next meeting?"** Had this motion to postpone till the next meeting been voted down, the next business would have been discussion on the motion to refer. Had this motion to refer been voted down the next business would have been discussion on the amendment. Had the amendment been voted down, the next business would have been discussion on the main motion. And during discussion on the main motion any member could have moved another amendment.

Clever opponents can delay a final vote on the motion as long as they please by clever debate and clever amendments unless the supporters of the main motion have a two-thirds vote and therefore can pass the motion "to close debate and vote immediately on all pending questions."

Of course, a majority vote in favor of the motion to adjourn would close the meeting at once. And a majority vote in favor of either the motion to lay on the table, the motion to postpone till the next meeting, the motion to refer or the motion to postpone indefinitely would immediately dispose of the main motion for the present together with all the motions pending that applied to the main motion, such as the amendment.

APPENDAGE MOTIONS (pages 16 and 19)

An amendment is a subsidiary motion, but it is a special form of subsidiary motion that may be called Appendage. An appendage motion is one that takes its rank from the motion to which it applies. Thus an amendment to the main motion takes precedence over the main motion but yields to all other motions. The amendment on page 16 is the "amendment to the main motion."

However, amendments may be made to the motion to refer, to the motion to postpone to a certain day and to the motion to limit debate. Obviously these motions could not be amended before they are voted on unless the motion to amend them took precedence over them. Therefore, the motion "to amend the main motion" does not have precedence over the motion to refer. But the motion "to amend the motion to refer" does take precedence over the motion to refer, but not over the motion to postpone to a certain day. Similarly the motion "to amend the motion to postpone to a certain day" must take precedence over the motion "to postpone to a certain day" but not over the "motion to close debate."

Thus the motion to amend is a special form of subsidiary motion called "appendage motion" because it has no absolute rank, but instead takes its rank from the motion to which it applies.

The motion to reconsider is the other appendage motion. Because it is an appendage motion and also has special rules as to who can move it and as to when it may be moved, the motion to reconsider is the most complicated of all motions. This motion is not classified at all in most manuals because it applies to the "vote" on the motion and not to the motion itself. However, it is as pure an example of the appendage principle as is the motion to amend in that it takes its precedence (and in fact most other features of its status) from the motion to which it applies.

Purpose, Precedence, and Strategic Use of Motions.

In the Appendix at the back of the manual is a brief explanation of the purpose, precedence, and strategic use of the more important motions.

HOW TO USE MANUAL

The Eight Phases of Each Motion.

Each motion has eight different phases or aspects that are indicated by the following eight questions.

1. May this motion apply to other motions?
2. May the mover of this motion interrupt another member who is speaking?
3. Must a member be recognized by the Chair before he can make this motion?
4. Must this motion be seconded before it is officially before the assembly?
5. Is this motion debatable?
6. What vote is required for its adoption?
7. May this motion be renewed after it has been voted down?
8. What other motions may apply to this motion?

Any good text on parliamentary procedure will answer all eight of these questions on each motion. But it would take the ordinary person many minutes, perhaps an hour, to find the answer to these eight questions on any one motion in these standard texts.

In this manual the answer to any one of these eight questions on any motion may be found in just two seconds by turning to this motion in the "finder index" at the center of the book and looking at the chart in the middle of that page. Thus under the main motion, page 18, will be found this chart.

1	2	3	4
May apply to the following motions	May interrupt a member who has the floor	Mover must first be recognized	Requires a second
No other motion	No	Yes	Yes

5	6	7	8
Debatable	Vote required	May be renewed	Motions that may apply to it
Yes	Majority	Not at same session	All

Here are the correct answers to these eight questions and these anwers will be found in exactly this order under each motion. Thus item number 5 is "Debatable" and the answer is "yes" for a main motion. It should not take very long to learn where to look on this chart for the answer to each question. And once this sequence is learned, the answer to any one of the eight questions about any one of the motions may be found in less than two seconds.

For instance, someone may ask, "Is the motion to refer debatable?" Open the manual to the center where the motions are listed in a finder-index, place your thumb on the page that is headed "To Refer," throw the manual open at that page (page 15), look at item 5 in the chart (first item on right hand page) and read:

	5	
	Debatable	
	Yes	

Thus the information is available in a second, it is in plain English, not in a code, and it is correct because these rules are in accordance with the Congressional Manual and other standard texts on Rules of Order (parliamentary procedure).

In brief, this manual eliminates the necessity for memorizing the many, many rules of parliamentary procedure, and permits the chairman to concentrate on maintaining order in the assembly and on making it clear to the assembly as to what is before them for consideration and vote. This manual also enables a member to check up on these rules in a second, before he makes a motion, to be sure that his motion is in order and that he is moving it in the proper manner.

Proper Phraseology

In addition to giving the rules of procedure for each motion, this manual also provides the proper form for stating each motion when a member is moving it, and the proper phrases for the chairman to use when restating the motion to the assembly, when putting it to a vote and when stating the result of an "Aye" vote or a "No" vote.

The phrase to be used by a member in making the motion is in ordinary type at the top of the left hand page following the word "Member." The phrases for the chairman to use are in bold-faced type on the left hand page following the word "Chairman."

Parliamentary Phrases for a Chairman

The amateur chairman will do well to read these phrases directly from the manual in handling any motion because these phrases are correct, they are complete, and they lead the chairman safely and quickly through the discussion, the vote, the result of the vote, and thence to what is next to come before the assembly.

A proud chairman should not disdain to use these mechanical aids because the Speaker of the United States House of Representatives has two parliamentary assistants to aid him in addition to the regular clerk of the House. The clerk on the speaker's left is called the time-keeper, and he keeps a check on time allotted to each member who speaks, but he helps in other ways, such as by identifying quickly congressmen who rise to speak. The clerk on the speaker's right is called the parliamentarian and it is his duty to check up on all fine points of procedure that arise, but he likewise helps to identify new members of Congress when they arise to speak.

Being a good chairman is a large undertaking and no chairman should neglect to use all the help he can find, because correctness is of first importance with a chairman, and correctness is a matter of fact not a matter of conceit.

APPENDIX

Purpose and Precedence of Motions

MAIN QUESTION (or Motion)

The main question or motion is the main idea before the group, such as a motion to have a dance or a motion to raise the dues. Obviously, it would lead to confusion to have members discussing two different ideas at the same time; hence the rule that only one main motion can be before the assembly at any one time, and the correlative rule that a main motion can not be introduced when any other motion is before the group.

AMENDMENTS

Amendments are for the purpose of changing a motion before that motion comes up for a final vote. Amendments may be quite difficult for a chairman to handle because they vary all the way from short, simple amendments to long, complicated ones; from clever, time-wasting amendments to ridiculous but well-meaning ones. Which to permit and which to declare out of order must be decided by the Chair promptly upon the basis of plain common sense. It is frequently quite difficult for the chairman to differentiate between the clever amendment with evil intent that frequently should be declared out of order, and the awkward but well-meaning amendment that should be permitted even though the secretary may have to re-word it in order that it may make sense. It is a part of the chairman's business to help the dumb or ignorant member formulate the amendment he has in mind but can not state in proper parliamentary form. On the other hand, it is equally important that the chairman prevent the smart-Aleck member from wasting the time of the assembly with well-formulated but purely obstructionist motions. Sound judgment and a forceful personality are both requisites of a first class chairman.

Another difficulty connected with amendments is the matter of their precedence, because an amendment is necessarily an "appendage" to another motion; consequently, it must always have precedence over the motion to which it applies. In the manual index it is given low precedence, but this is only for amendments to the main motion, and the main motion has the lowest precedence of all the motions. Obviously, an amendment to the motion to refer must have precedence over the motion to refer. Likewise, an amendment to the motion to limit debate must have precedence over the motion to limit debate. Finally, if no time has been fixed for the next meeting and some one moves that the "time for the next meeting be Friday evening," then an amendment to this motion "fixing the time for the next meeting" must of necessity have precedence over **all other motions.** This is so because the motion "to fix the time for the next meeting" (when no such time has yet been fixed) takes precedence over all other motions, and an amendment to it must of necessity have precedence over it. Hence the rule that an amendment takes precedence over the motion to which it applies, so that its absolute precedence is simply that of the motion to which it applies. In short, it is an appendage motion.

MOTION TO RECONSIDER

The motion to reconsider is another "appendage" motion that takes its precedence from the motion to which it applies. Thus the motion to **"reconsider the vote on the motion to close debate"** must be acted on at once because you can not proceed with the business before the assembly until you have finally settled the question as to whether you are or are not going to close debate. Obviously, the motion to reconsider suspends action on the motion to which it applies until the motion to reconsider has been acted on. For this reason the motion to reconsider must be acted on at once if it applies to the motion to close debate. But it need not be acted on at once if it applies to the main motion or to a subsidiary motion that does not require immediate action.

An especially difficult feature of the motion to reconsider is that it has one precedence for entry (for moving it) and another precedence for actual consideration and vote. The reason for this difference in the precedence of two different phases of the same motion is that the motion to reconsider is in order **only for a brief period,** usually not more than one day after the vote on the motion to which it applies. Consequently, the motion to reconsider must be moved when it is still in order. If certain other business is before the assembly when you decide that you would like to move reconsideration on a motion that was voted on yesterday, this other business before the assembly may not be disposed of until after the time for moving reconsideration of yesterday's motion has expired. It is in view of this frequent possibility that a member is permitted to "interrupt other business," may even "interrupt a member who has the floor and is speaking" in order to move reconsideration on a motion that has already been moved on. However, when the motion to reconsider has been moved and therefore entered on the minutes, it need not be acted on at once, because it automatically suspends action on the motion to which it applies.

When a pending question is interrupted by a member who desires to move reconsideration on a former main motion, this pending question is resumed immediately after the interruption and disposed of. Then, when there is no other business before the assembly, this motion to reconsider, previously moved, should be taken up and disposed of. For consideration and vote the motion to reconsider has only the precedence of the motion to which it applies; consequently, if it applies to a main motion it can only be taken up for consideration and vote when there is no other business before the assembly. But (for the reasons given above) the motion to reconsider the vote on a former main motion has high privilege for entry (that is, to be moved).

Reconsideration of an affirmative vote on a subsidiary motion has much the same status as reconsideration of a main motion, because such an affirmative vote disposes of the main motion temporarily at least, and, therefore, this reconsideration is much the same as reconsideration of the vote on the main motion itself. Thus reconsideration of an affirmative vote on the motion to refer brings both the motion to refer and the main motion back before the assembly for consideration. However, reconsideration of an affirmative vote on the motion to close debate must be moved immediately after the vote on the motion to close debate because obviously there would be no point to moving reconsideration on the motion to close debate after the main motion had been disposed of. (The motion to close debate provides for an immediate vote on the pending question.)

A negative vote on a subsidiary, incidental, or privileged motion can not be reconsidered except immediately after the vote is taken for the obvious reason that " after progress" these subsidiary, incidental, and privileged motions may, as a rule, be "renewed." Thus when the motion to close debate has been voted down and then debate has proceeded for some time, the way to close debate is not by moving reconsideration of the former vote on the motion to close debate. On the contrary, the quickest and least confusing way is simply to move again that "debate be closed," since this motion may be "renewed" after progress.

CLINCHING THE MOTION (by Reconsideration)

A common parliamentary trick called "clinching the motion" involves the use of the motion to reconsider, but in this case the motion to reconsider is moved, not by one who has suddenly changed his mind about the motion just voted on, but by one who voted with the majority and wants to "clinch" this majority victory before some member of the majority does change his mind. Immediately after the majority passes or defeats a motion the majority leader moves that this vote be reconsidered. Then the majority votes down the motion to reconsider so that if, later, some members of the majority do change their minds about the main motion that was voted on, they can not then move reconsideration because the rule is that "No motion may be twice reconsidered." Also, this method is used when a motion is passed by the assembly which should go into effect at once. Since the law can not be put into effect so long as the motion to reconsider may be moved, the way to speed its being put into effect is for the majority to move reconsideration immediately and then vote down reconsideration.

The minority frequently use the motion to reconsider as a means of delaying final action on a motion, but the majority can forestall this use of the motion by moving it themselves and then immediately voting it down. "What is sauce for the goose is sauce for the gander." (The motion to reconsider may be moved only by those who voted with the prevailing side, but this difficulty is easily solved by the minority by the simple device of having two members of the minority vote with the majority in order thus to qualify themselves to move and second the motion to reconsider.)

ADJOURNMENT

The motion to adjourn is one of the most common motions and one of the most highly privileged, provided the time for the next meeting is already determined, as it usually is in most organizations. When privileged, the motion to adjourn can be moved at almost any time and must be voted on at once because it is not debatable when privileged. However, the motion to adjourn is not privileged when no time has been fixed for the next meeting, because adjournment without time being fixed for the next meeting simply breaks up the organization, dissolves the assembly. When not privileged, the motion to adjourn can be moved only when there is no other business before the assembly, and in that case it is debatable. Also, in such a case, the motion to adjourn yields to the motion "to fix the time for the next meeting," for obvious reasons.

QUESTIONS OF PRIVILEGE

A common point for confusion is the difference between a question of privilege and a privileged question or motion. A question of privilege has to do with the rights and comforts of the assembly as a whole, or the rights and comfort of any member. As such, these rights are given immediate consideration regardless of what else is before the assembly. Thus if the room becomes too hot, a member may even interrupt a speaker in order to ask the chairman to provide adequate ventilation. When a motion is before the assembly and certain points of a confidential nature are brought up, any member may "rise to a question of privilege," and when the chairman says, "State your question of privilege," the member may say, "As a question of privilege I move that the visitors be asked to leave the room while this confidential matter is being discussed." If the chairman decides that conditions warrant granting this privilege he says, "As a question of privilege it is moved and seconded that the visitors be asked to leave the room while this confidential matter is being discussed. Is there any discussion on this privileged motion?"

The question of whether a member may demand better ventilation or may ask to be excused from the remainder of the meeting are questions of privilege. It is also a question of privilege when a member asks permission to interrupt a speaker and move that the room be cleared of visitors, or that the assembly go immediately to another room where it is warmer or where the light is better. Thus it is a question of privilege when another member asks permission to do something or to have something done which he could not do or could not have done under the ordinary rules of procedure. And the Chair decides immediately the point as to whether or not this special privilege is to be granted. Such a grant of privilege does not require any vote unless some member appeals from the decision of the Chair. (See Appeals, page 6.)

If, however, this question of privilege involves the right to make a motion and this privilege is granted by the Chair, then the motion made under this grant of special privilege becomes a **privileged motion** that must be disposed of by vote before the assembly can proceed with the business that was before it when this question of privilege was raised.

PRIVILEGED MOTIONS

A privileged motion is a motion of such a nature that it must be disposed of immediately, regardless of the other business that may be pending. The privileged motions are:—to fix the time for the next meeting (when no such time has been fixed); to adjourn (when privileged), (See above under Adjournment); to call for orders of the day (when there are such orders); and motions made under the grant of privilege by the Chair to a member who has "risen to a question of privilege."

RISING TO A POINT OF ORDER

Whenever a member believes that the Chair has made a mistake or a wrong decision, the member may rise to a point of order by saying as he rises (and without waiting to be recognized by the Chair), "Mr. Chairman, I rise to a point of order." This may even interrupt another member who has the floor and is speaking. The chairman should then say, "State your point of order." When the member states the point of order, the chairman decides, "Your point is **not** well taken," and then proceeds with whatever business is before the assembly, or he decides, "Your point is well taken," and then proceeds with whatever business is in order under the **reversed** ruling.

APPEALS

If any member is dissatisfied with any decision made by the Chair, he may appeal from this decision of the Chair **to the assembly** by rising and saying (without waiting to be recognized), "I appeal from the decision of the Chair." An appeal requires a second. One disgruntled member is not enough to warrant a vote of the assembly on a decision of the Chair. When there is such an appeal, the chairman states the reasons for his decision (if he desires to give reasons), and then calls for a vote by saying, "Those in favor of sustaining the decision of the Chair say 'Aye'. Those opposed to sustaining the decision of the Chair say 'No'." (See under motion to Appeal, page 6.)

DILATORY APPEALS

However, the Chair usually refuses to permit an appeal when the purpose of the appeal is obviously to delay action or to annoy the chairman. Here, as in every other act, the chairman must maintain his position of fairness and impartiality. It seldom pays to "steam roll" the minority even though the chairman knows that he has the undivided support of the majority. Common sense is the essence of parliamentary rules; fairplay is their guiding principle; reasonable discussion followed by prompt action is what they are devised to achieve.

OBJECTION TO CONSIDERATION

Objection to consideration is a motion that is not often used, but it is invaluable when needed. Its purpose is to prevent any discussion on a motion when either the motion or the discussion on it is quite objectionable to a large majority of the group. Since its purpose is to eliminate undesirable motions, it applies only to the main motion and to questions of privilege, because these are the only two methods of bringing unexpected subjects before the assembly. Also, since its further purpose is to prevent any discussion on this undesirable motion, a member may interrupt a speaker in order to move "objection to consideration." And since only one member may know of the evil involved in the undesirable motion, the motion "objection to consideration" does not require a second. However, two-thirds of the members must be against consideration in order thus to eliminate a motion without any discussion whatsoever. (For the phrasing of this difficult question and putting it to a vote see page 11, under "Objection to Consideration.") One little point in this connection that may easily be overlooked in the manual is that the motion to lay on the table is out of order immediately after "objection to consideration" has been defeated. That is to say, when one more than one-third of the assembly vote in favor of "considering the motion" (It takes a two-thirds vote in the negative to prevent consideration), it is not then permissible for a bare majority of 51 per cent to lay aside the motion objected to, without any discussion, by means of the motion to lay on the table which is not debatable and requires only a majority vote. However, after there has been several minutes of discussion on the undesirable motion, the motion to lay on the table is in order and may be applied. Stated briefly, if objection to consideration is moved against a certain motion and one more than one-third of the assembly vote in favor of considering the motion, then a few minutes of discussion must be permitted on the undesirable motion before it is disposed of.

The question may well be asked, "Why not move to lay on the

XXIV

(Continued to back of Manual, page xxv)

Member:—"Mr. Chairman" (Pause for recognition) "I move that when this assembly adjourns, it adjourn to meet (state the time) in (name the place, if necessary)."

Chairman:—"It is moved and seconded that when this assembly adjourns, it adjourn to meet (state the time) (and if necessary, the place). Is there any discussion?" (See 4, opposite page.)

Put to VOTE:—"The vote is on the motion that when this assembly adjourns, it adjourn to meet (state time and place). Those in favor of fixing the time for the next meeting at (state time and place) say 'Aye'. (Pause) Those opposed say 'No'."

"Aye" vote:—"The 'Ayes' have it, and the motion fixing the time for the next meeting is carried. The next meeting will be held at (state time and place). Is there any other business?" (Consult secretary as to next business.)

"No" vote:—"The 'Noes' have it and the motion to fix the time for the next meeting is lost. Is there any other business?" (Consult secretary.)

1	2	3	4
May apply to the following motions	May interrupt a member who has the floor	Mover must first be recognized	Requires a second
None	No	Yes	Yes

Note:—Ordinarily, the motion to fix the time for the next meeting is just a main motion such as "I move that the next meeting be at seven-thirty, next Wednesday night instead of the usual time, eight-thirty." This motion has no privilege because there will be a meeting next Wednesday at eight-thirty even though the above motion is never moved, or, having been moved, is defeated.

But, if there is no time fixed for the next meeting, the motion to adjourn puts an end not only to this meeting but also to any future meetings. Consequently, when no time is fixed for the next meeting, the motion "to fix the time for the next meeting" is the most highly privileged of all motions and can be moved even after the motion to adjourn has been moved, seconded and voted on, provided the Chair has not yet declared the meeting adjourned. Of course the meeting is over and no further business can be transacted once the Chair, if properly authorized, declares the meeting adjourned.

1. When privileged (see 6) takes precedence of all other motions except a motion to recess already pending.

2. Is in order even after a vote to adjourn if the result of the vote has not yet been announced by the Chair.

3. May be amended, but only by altering the time or place (or both) at which meeting shall be held.

4. Not debatable when another motion is before the assembly.

5. Not subject to subsidiary motions except amendment. (See 3.)

6. Has no privilege when time has already been fixed for next regular meeting.

5	6	7	8
Debatable	Vote required	May be renewed	Motions that may apply to it
Not when privileged (See 4 and 6)	Majority	Not for same time	Amend, reconsider

However, when there is need for another meeting, or when there is necessity for changing the time of the next meeting, the Chair should call attention to this necessity if the motion to adjourn is moved before the time for the next meeting has been determined.

When no time has been fixed for the next meeting, the motion to adjourn is not privileged (see rules on "to adjourn" page 2) and therefore, is not in order when any other motion is pending. In short, the motion to adjourn is just an ordinary main motion when no time has been fixed for the next meeting.

The general belief that the motion to adjourn is "always in order and not debatable" is based on the fact that in nearly all organizations the time is fixed for the next meeting and therefore, the motion to adjourn is highly privileged and is not debatable.

Member:—"Mr. Chairman" (Pause for recognition) "I move that we adjourn."

Chairman:—"It is moved and seconded that we adjourn. Those in favor of adjournment say 'Aye'. (Pause) Those opposed say 'No'."

"Aye" vote:—"The 'Ayes' have it, and the motion to adjourn is carried. You stand adjourned." (Sound gavel.)

"No" vote:—"The 'Noes' have it and the motion to adjourn is lost. The next business is (consult secretary)."
Or, Is there further discussion on (state motion before assembly when it was moved to adjourn).

1	2	3	4
May apply to the following motions	May interrupt a member who has the floor	Mover must first be recognized	Requires a second
None	No	Yes	Yes

IN COMMITTEE:—When a committee finishes its business it should "rise" or "rise and report." However, a committee may "adjourn" from time to time till its business is completed.

1. When unqualified, takes precedence of all motions except to fix time for next meeting.
2. When qualified, it is without privilege.
3. Is in order even after vote ordered on main question.
4. Debatable only when not privileged (see 7), or when adjournment would constitute a dissolution of the assembly.
5. Renewable, but only after some progress.
6. A special order fixing the time for adjournment takes precedence over everything. But this special order may be postponed by a two-thirds vote.
7. Not privileged when no time has been fixed for next meeting.
8. Not debatable when privileged.
9. Cannot be reconsidered, amended or have any other subsidiary motion applied to it if it is unqualified.
10. Quorum is not required for its adoption.
11. It is not always in order. May not interrupt a speaker or the verification of a vote; may not be entertained during a division, nor be renewed until some progress has been made.

5	6	7	8
Debatable	Vote required	May be renewed	Motions that may apply to it
Not when privileged	Majority (See 10)	Yes, after progress	None

TO RECESS:—A motion to Recess for a short period has no precedence unless proposed as an urgent question of privilege. (See Question of Privilege, page 3.)

Member:—"Mr. Chairman" (Pause for recognition) "I move that we recess (state time of recess or duration)." Note:—It is also advisable to state reasons for having a recess.

The rules are the same as "To Adjourn." When the time for the Recess has expired, the Chair again calls the meeting to order and resumes the business of the meeting that was pending (if any) when the Recess began.

Member:—"Mr. Chairman, I rise to a question of privilege."

Chairman:—"Please state your question."

Member:—"I request that the speaker be asked to go to the front of the room so all can hear him."

Chairman:—"Your privilege is granted. Will the speaker please come to the front of the room?"

Question of Privilege and Privileged Motion

Member:—"I rise to a question of privilege."

Chairman:—"Please state your question."

Member:—"As a question of privilege I move that the visitors be asked to leave the room till this business is concluded."

Chairman:—"Your privilege is granted. As a question of privilege it has been moved and seconded that the visitors be asked to leave the room till this business is concluded. Is there any discussion on this privileged motion? etc."

1	2	3	4
May apply to the following motions	May interrupt a member who has the floor	Mover must first be recognized	Requires a second
None	Yes, if necessary	No	No

PRIVILEGED MOTION resulting from a Question of Privilege.

Chairman:—"It is moved and seconded that (state motion that was given privileged status under Question of Privilege). Is there any discussion on this privileged motion?"

Put to VOTE:—(Same as any other motion.)

"Aye" vote:—"The 'Ayes' have it, and the privileged motion is carried." (Chairman should take whatever action is required by the adoption of this privileged motion.) Then chairman should go immediately back to the pending question, be it the main motion or a subsidiary motion.

"No" vote:—"The 'Noes' have it and the privileged motion is lost. Is there further discussion on the (state the question or motion that was pending when the Question of Privilege was raised)."

1. Takes precedence of all other motions except to adjourn and to fix time of next meeting.

2. Questions of privilege (of the first class) that affect the honor, dignity or safety of the assembly are superior to those (of the second class) that concern only individuals. See below.

3. May interrupt a speaker if immediate action is required.

4. Are decided by the Chair subject to appeal to the assembly.

5. May be disposed of by any subsidiary motion, but such subsidiary motion affects only the question of privilege or the resulting privileged motion, not the main question.

6. Final action need not be taken at once.

7. Chair decides only whether question is one of privilege;—not, usually, as to the particular action required. If question is decided to be a question of privilege (by the Chair or by the assembly on appeal), it has then acquired the status of a privileged motion, but see rule 6 above.

Chart for Questions of Privilege, NOT resulting Privileged Motions.

5	6	7	8
Debatable	Vote required	May be renewed	Motions that may apply to it
No, but a resulting motion is	Decided by Chair (See 4)	After progress	None apply to question of privilege, but all may apply to resulting privileged motion

EXAMPLES:—Questions of privilege of first class involve disorder in the gallery, tampering with papers, bad heating or ventilating, etc.

Questions of privilege of second class involve personal threats or attacks, illness, desire to be excused, etc.

Member:—"Mr. Chairman, I call for the order of the day."

Chairman:—"**If there is no objection, the order of the day will now be taken up.**" (Secretary has record of the orders.)

(If called for at the proper time, a special order must be taken up unless there is objection in the form of a two-thirds vote in favor of postponement.)

To Postpone a Special Order

Member:—"Mr. Chairman" (Pause for recognition) "I move that we postpone this special order till the business now before the assembly is concluded (or 'for twenty minutes' or 'till the next meeting')."

Chairman:—(if motion is seconded) "**It is moved and seconded that we postpone this special order until the business now before the assembly is concluded. Those in favor of postponement say 'Aye'.** (Pause) **Those opposed say 'No'.**"

"Aye" vote:—"The 'Ayes' have it by a two-thirds vote, and the special order is postponed until the business now before the assembly is concluded. Is there any further discussion on the motion (state the motion already before the assembly when the order of the day was called for)?"

"No" vote:—"**The 'Noes' have it by more than a one-third vote and the motion to postpone the special order is lost. The next business is the special order for today at this time** (state the motion or business that was made the special order for this time)."

To Call for Order of the Day

1	2	3	4
May apply to the following motions	May interrupt a member who has the floor	Mover must first be recognized	Requires a second
Any special or general order	Yes, to call for a special order (See 2 and 11)	No	No

1. Takes precedence of all other motions except to adjourn and questions of privilege.

2. May interrupt a speaker to call for a special order, but not for a general order.

3. To be privileged, the call must be for the orders generally, not for any particular one.

4. A general order may be postponed by a majority vote.

5. A special order may be postponed by a two-thirds vote.

6. Orders of the Day may be taken up by the Chair without a motion or a vote if no one objects.

7. Does not require a second.

8. Is not debatable or amendable.

9. Motion to take up part of the orders has no privilege.

10. If not taken up at the time specified, the order is nullified.

11. A later special order cannot supercede or interfere with another special order previously assigned.

12. General orders cannot interfere with established rules.

13. A call for the orders cannot be renewed until the pending question is disposed of.

To Call for Order of the Day

5	6	7	8
Debatable	Vote required	May be renewed	Motions that may apply to it
No	None, it takes ⅔ vote to postpone special order	Yes, but (See 13)	None, except to postpone orders

(Parliamentary Inquiry)   (For Information)

Member:— (Rising, but not waiting to be recognized.) "Mr. Chairman, I rise to a point of order."

Chairman:—"State your point of order."

Member:—"The motion just proposed is out of order because there is already a main motion before the assembly."

Chairman:—"Your point is well taken. The motion last proposed is out of order."

OR—"Your point is not well taken. (If a member speaking was interrupted by this point of order the chairman should tell that member to resume speaking.) The speaker will please continue."

Rising to a Point of Order, Parliamentary Inquiry, or Information

1	2	3	4
May apply to the following motions	May interrupt a member who has the floor	Mover must first be recognized	Requires a second
Any motion or act	Yes	No	No

Rising to a Parliamentary Inquiry

1. If the Chair cannot answer the inquiry, he may refer it to the parliamentarian or to some member of the assembly.

2. A parliamentary inquiry may not lead to **debate,** nor to an **appeal.**

Member:—"Mr. Chairman, I rise to a parliamentary inquiry."

Chairman:—"State your inquiry."

Member:—"Is it in order to offer an amendment now?"

Chairman:—"It is."

1. May interrupt a speaker, or even a vote if need be.
2. The point of order is decided by the Chair.
   (a) If dissatisfied with the decision of the Chair any member may APPEAL to the assembly for a final decision.
   Form of APPEAL:—"I appeal from the decision of the Chair."
   (An appeal requires a second.) (See appeals, page 6.)
3. Chair may briefly state the reasons for his decision.
4. If Chair is in doubt as to the point of order he may refer it to a vote of the assembly for final decision.
5. A member having the floor when point of order is raised, must take his seat until the point of order is decided.
6. A point of order must be raised immediately after the error has been made except in the case of a clear violation of the constitution or by-laws.
7. Does not require a second and is not debatable.
8. No other motion may apply to it.

5	6	7	8
Debatable	Vote required (Point of order only)	May be renewed	Motions that may apply to it
No, but see appeals	None, unless appealed, then majority	No	None but see appeals

Rising for Information

1. All requests for information are addressed to the Chair even though aimed at another member.

2. All anwers to questions are addressed to the Chair.
   (a) Direct controversies between members are an affront to the dignity of the assembly.

3. A member rising too often should not be given recognition by the Chair.

Member:—"Mr. Chairman, I rise for information," or "I should like to ask the gentleman a question."

Chairman:—"State your question." In second inquiry chairman asks the member speaking from the floor if he is willing to be interrupted. If he is, the chairman then turns to the member who rose for information and says:—"State your question." (See 1 and 2 above.)

Member:—"Mr. Chairman, I appeal from the decision of the Chair."

Chairman:—"There is an appeal from the decision of the Chair. (If debatable, Is there any discussion?) Those in favor of sustaining the decision of the Chair say 'Aye'. (Pause) Those opposed to sustaining the decision of the Chair say 'No'."

"Aye" vote:—"The 'Ayes' have it, and the decision of the Chair is sustained." (Tell the assembly what is next in order.)

"No" vote:— "The 'Noes' have it and the decision of the Chair is reversed by the vote of the assembly." (Tell the assembly what is next in order under this reversed ruling.)

No Appeal on Questions of Dilatory Motions

"The object of a parliamentary body is action, not stoppage of action." Therefore, the Speaker of the United States House of Representatives has declined to entertain debate or appeal on question as to dilatoriness of a motion, because to do so would be to nullify the rule; but he has recognized that the authority conferred by the rule should not be exercised until the object of the dilatory motion "becomes apparent to the house." Usually, but not always, the Speaker "awaits a point of order from the floor before acting." (Rules of House of Representatives of U.S. 71st Congress, 1929, page 346, section 785.)

1	2	3	4
May apply to the following motions	May interrupt a member who has the floor	Mover must first be recognized	Requires a second
Any decision by the Chair	Yes (See 7)	No	Yes

1. Must be seconded.

2. Takes precedence of the question which gives rise to it.

3. Is in order even when another member has the floor.

4. Yields to adjournment, questions of privilege, and orders of the day.

5. Subject to motion to table and to close debate, if debatable.

   (a) Effect of motion to table in this connection is to "kill the appeal without debate" and thus sustain the decision of the Chair without a direct vote on the appeal.

6. A tie vote on an appeal sustains the decision of the Chair.

7. Not in order unless made immediately after decision by the Chair.

8. Not in order when another appeal is pending. (Chair's decisions are final on all points of order raised while an appeal is pending.)

9. Not debatable if made when an undebatable motion is pending.

10. Not debatable if appeal relates only to decorum, to violation of the rules, or to order of business.

11. Cannot be amended.

12. If debate is closed on the appeal or the appeal is tabled, this action does not affect the main motion pending.

5	6	7	8
Debatable	Vote required	May be renewed	Motions that may apply to it
No (See 5, 9, 10)	Majority	No	To lay on table, to close debate, reconsider

Member:—"Mr. Chairman" (Pause for recognition) "I move to suspend the rules which interfere with (specify the items interfered with by present rules)."

Chairman:—"It is moved and seconded that we suspend the rules which interfere with (specify items interfered with by rules). Those in favor of suspension of these rules say 'Aye'. (Pause) Those opposed to suspension of these rules say 'No'."

"Aye" vote:—"The 'Ayes' have it by a two-thirds vote, and the motion to suspend the rules is carried." (State the next business under suspension of the rules.)

"No" vote:—"The 'Noes' have it by more than a one-third vote and the motion to suspend the rules is lost." (State the next business under the rules.)

1	2	3	4
May apply to the following motions	May interrupt a member who has the floor	Mover must first be recognized	Requires a second
Any motion where needed	No	Yes	Yes

1. Takes precedence of the main motion and all subsidiary motions, but yields to all privileged motions.

2. Requires two-thirds vote unless otherwise specified in the constitution or by-laws.

3. Rules can be suspended **only** when they make provision for such suspension, and then only in accordance with such provisions.

4. The motion to suspend the rules is exhausted on the one purpose specified in the motion.

5. Cannot be debated.

6. Cannot have any subsidiary motion apply to it.

7. Cannot be reconsidered.

8. Cannot be renewed for the same purpose, except at a later meeting.

5	6	7	8
Debatable	Vote required	May be renewed	Motions that may apply to it
No	Usually ⅔ See Constitution	No, except by unanimous consent	None

As a Subsidiary Motion

(To Postpone to Certain Day)

For example:—When Report of Committee on By-Laws is before the Assembly.

Member:—"Mr. Chairman" (Pause for recognition) "I move that we postpone consideration of this report till Friday at 3 P.M. and make it a special order for that time."

Chairman:—"It is moved and seconded that we postpone consideration of the By-Laws Committee Report till Friday at 3 P.M. and make it a special order for that time. Is there any discussion either on the postponement or on making it a special order for that time?" (Requires two-thirds vote.)

Put to VOTE:—"The vote is on the motion to postpone the By-Laws Committee Report till Friday at 3 P.M. and make it a special order for that time. Those in favor say 'Aye'. (Pause) Those opposed say 'No'."

"Aye" vote:—"The 'Ayes' have it by a two-thirds vote, and the motion is carried to postpone till Friday at 3 P.M. and create a special order for that time. Is there any other business?"

"No" vote:—"The 'Noes' have it by more than a one-third vote and the motion to postpone definitely and create a special order is lost. Is there any further discussion on the Report of the Committee on By-Laws?"

Chart for Motion to Create a Special Order

1	2	3	4
May apply to the following motions	May interrupt a member who has the floor	Mover must first be recognized	Requires a second
Main motion	No	Yes	Yes

To Create General Order

1. Requires majority vote only.
2. Cannot interfere with established rules.
3. In all other ways same as motion to create special orders.

1. May be made as a main motion or as motion to postpone to certain day.
2. Requires two-thirds majority whether as main or subsidiary motion.
3. At the time specified a special order takes precedence of any interfering general order. (See Orders of Day 1, 2, 5, 9 and 11 on page 4R.)
4. Has no privilege over ordinary main motion or motion to postpone to certain day.

As a Main Motion

Member:—"Mr. Chairman" (Pause for recognition) "I move that (the report of the Committee on By-Laws) be made a special order for (Friday at 3 P.M.)."

Chairman:—"It is moved and seconded that (the report of the By-Laws Committee) be made a special order for (Friday at 3 P.M.). Is there any discussion?"

Put to VOTE:—"The vote is on the motion that the (report of the By-Laws Committee) be made a special order for (Friday at 3 P.M.). Those in favor say 'Aye'. (Pause) Those opposed say 'No'." (Requires two-thirds vote.)

"Aye" vote:—"The 'Ayes' have it by a two-thirds vote, and the special order is carried. (The report of the By-Laws Committee) will be a special order for (Friday at 3 P.M.). Is there any other business?"

"No" vote:—"The 'Noes' have it by more than a one-third vote and the motion to create a special order is lost. Is there any other business?"

5	6	7	8
Debatable	Vote required	May be renewed	Motions that may apply to it
Yes	⅔	After progress	All

Orders of the day once created have status of established rules and, therefore, can be changed only by a two-thirds vote same as "suspension of rules."

Chair should bring up motions (ordered by motion to create general or special orders) at the time ordered. If he fails to do so, any member may "call for orders of the day." (See motion "to call for orders of the day" page 4.)

To Withdraw A Motion

Member:—who made the original motion—"Mr. Chairman" (Pause for recognition) "I desire to withdraw my motion."

Chairman:—"Mr. X asks leave to withdraw his motion. If there is no objection, the motion will be withdrawn. Is there any other business?"

If any member objects to the withdrawal, some other member should rise, be recognized, and move:—

Other Member:—"Mr Chairman" (Pause for recognition) "I move that Mr. X be allowed to withdraw his motion."

Chairman:—"It is moved that Mr. X be allowed to withdraw his motion. Those in favor say 'Aye'. (Pause) Those opposed say 'No'."

"Aye" vote:—"The 'Ayes' have it, and Mr. X has permission to withdraw his motion. Is there any other business?"

"No" vote:—"The 'Noes' have it and permission to withdraw the motion before the assembly is denied. Is there any further discussion on Mr. X's motion that we (state the motion)."

Chart of Motion to Permit Withdrawal of a Motion

1	2	3	4
May apply to the following motions	May interrupt a member who has the floor	Mover must first be recognized	Requires a second
Any motion	No	Yes	No

TO RENEW A MOTION (There is no "motion to renew a motion").

a. A main question cannot be renewed except by motion to reconsider or to take from the table.

b. An amendment cannot be renewed in the same form if objection is made except by the motion to reconsider.

1. A main motion may be withdrawn (by the mover) at any time before final action is reached, provided no one objects.

2. If objection is made, leave to withdraw may be granted by a motion to that effect moved by another member.

3. Cannot be debated or amended.

Chart of Motion to Permit Withdrawal of a Motion

5	6	7	8
Debatable	Vote required	May be renewed	Motions that may apply to it
No	Majority	After progress	Reconsider

TO RENEW A MOTION

1. Any privileged motion, any incidental motion except objection to consideration and suspension of the rules for an incidental purpose, and any subsidiary motion except a specific amendment (see b, opposite page) may be renewed after progress in business has altered the former state of affairs.

10 VOTING—"DIVISION"—MOTION TO BALLOT

The usual method of voting is by **sound** (called viva voce voting). This is quick, convenient, but not accurate for a close vote.

A show of hands is likewise quick and convenient, but not accurate for a close vote.

CALLING FOR A DIVISION. After a vote by **sound** (or, in a large assembly by **show of hands)** any member may "call for a division" of vote, that is, a vote that can be accurately counted: rising vote, roll call or an actual "division."

Member:—"Mr. Chairman, I call for a division!" Or, without rising the member may simply call out "DIVISION!"

Chairman:—"A division is called for. Those in favor of the motion please stand. (After counting) Be seated. Those opposed please stand. (After counting) Be seated."

If the chairman himself is in doubt as to an "Aye" and "No" vote, he should say, **"The Chair is in doubt. Those in favor of this motion please rise** (or raise the right hand)," etc.

"AYE" vs. "I"—In this manual the adverb meaning "yes" is spelled "Aye." Common usage is to spell it "Aye" and pronounce it "I."

Rules

1. Vote by ballot may be ordered by a motion to that effect, provided it is not already required by the Constitution or By-Laws.

2. Motion to ballot (or vote by roll call) is not debatable.

3. When balloting is ordered, Chair should appoint two or more tellers to conduct the vote by distributing, collecting and counting the ballots.

Member:—"Mr. Chairman" (Pause for recognition) "I move that the vote on this question be by ballot."

Chairman:—"It is moved and seconded that the vote on this question be by ballot. Those in favor of voting by ballot say 'Aye'. (Pause) Those opposed to voting by ballot say 'No'."

"Aye" vote:—"The 'Ayes' have it, and the motion to ballot is carried. I appoint Mr. ——, Mr. —— and Mr. —— as tellers to distribute, collect and count the ballots."

"No" vote:—"The 'Noes' have it and the motion to vote by ballot is lost. The next business is (whatever motion is immediately pending)." (Consult secretary if in doubt.)

Tellers Report:—The tellers should hand to the secretary a written tabulation of the vote just as soon as possible.

Member:— (Rising, but not waiting to be recognized) "Mr. Chairman, I object to the consideration of this motion!"

NOTE:—Never put a motion in negative form.

Chairman:—"There is objection to the consideration of this motion. Those in favor of considering this motion say 'Aye'. (Pause) Those opposed to considering this motion say 'No'."

"Aye" vote:—"The 'Ayes' have it by more than a one-third vote, and the motion will be considered. Is there any discussion on the motion that we (state the original motion)?" (Go to page 18, left, **Put To VOTE** phrase next.)

"No" vote:—**"The 'Noes' have it by a two-thirds vote and the motion that we** (state original motion) **will not be considered. Is there any other business?"**

1	2	3	4
May apply to the following motions	May interrupt a member who has the floor	Movers must first be recognized	Requires a second
Main question, and questions of privilege	Yes	No	No

1. Applies only to main motion and to questions of privilege.

2. Is in order only when question is first introduced and before debate.

3. May interrupt a member speaking.

4. Requires a two-thirds vote in the negative (two-thirds vote against consideration).

5. Chairman himself may raise the question of consideration.

6. Requires no second.

7. Cannot be debated or amended.

8. If more than one-third of assembly votes in favor of consideration, then the motion to lay on the table is not immediately in order.

5	6	7	8
Debatable	Vote required	May be renewed	Motions that may apply to it
No	⅔ in negative	No	Reconsider

INDEX

Index for Parliamentary Procedure

INDEX (Cont'd)

Index for Parliamentary Procedure

a. **Chairman:**—(Sounds gavel) **"The meeting will come to order."** (When members have become quiet) **"The secretary will read the minutes of the last meeting."** (Or, Business is now in order).

(After reading of the minutes)

b. **Chairman:**—**"Are there any objections to or corrections of the minutes?"** (Pause) **"If not, the minutes will stand approved as read. The next business is ———."**

(If there is disagreement in the assembly as to a certain correction, this point of correction should be put to a vote of the assembly to settle it officially.)

c. ORDERS OF THE DAY. (See pages 4 and 8.)
(If, for example, the report of the finance committee had been made a special order for this meeting) :—

Chairman:—**"The report of the finance committee was made a special order for this meeting. The chairman of the finance committee will read his report."** (See 5, opposite page for handling reports and committee recommendations.)

d. ADJOURNMENT. **Chairman:**—**"If there is no further business, a motion to adjourn is in order."** (See page 2.)

(If adjournment has been previously ordered at a set time, say at 10 P. M., the Chair adjourns the meeting automatically at the time specified.)

Chairman:—**"It is now ten o'clock. You stand adjourned."** (Chairman sounds gavel and the meeting is ended.)

Each organization has the right to determine whether it shall have any fixed order of business, and, if so, what that order shall be.

Usual Order of Business

1. Calling meeting to order.   (See a, opposite page.)

2. Reading and approval of minutes.   (See b, opposite page.)

3. Reports of committees.
   a. Standing committees.
   b. Special committees.   (See pages 13 and 8.)
      (The motion "to accept the report" should be made by a person not on the committee. If, however, the report recommends certain action by the entire organization, the chairman of the committee should make the necessary motion immediately after reading the report that recommends such action.)

4. Orders of the day, if any.   (See c, opposite page, also pages 4 and 20.)
   a. Special orders.   (See pages 4 and 8.)

5. Unfinished business.   (See minutes of last meeting.)
   a. General orders.   (See pages 13 and 20.)

6. New Business.

7. Adjournment.   (However, the motion to adjourn is almost always in order.)

Voting by Chairman:—A chairman who is at the same time a member in full standing can vote on any motion. He can even speak on any motion by asking someone to preside while he takes the floor.

The Vice-President of the United States can not vote on every motion because he is not a senator. He can vote in case of a tie because the Constitution gives him that special privilege.

A wise chairman does not vote when his vote would not be decisive simply because as the umpire of the contest between the proponents and the opponents his task is easier when he refuses to take sides in the controversy.

a. An office must be created by the Constitution or by a motion to that effect before it can be filled by election or otherwise.

b. The Chair must call for nominations.

Chairman:—**"Nominations are now in order for the office of —."**

c. Nominations do not require a second. However, any number of persons may second a given nomination just to show their support of that nominee.

Member:—"Mr. Chairman" (Pause for recognition) "I nominate Mr. George Smith for president."

Chairman:—**"Mr. George Smith is nominated. Are there other nominations?"** (After a pause) **"If not, the motion to close nominations is in order."**

d. The motion "to close nominations" is not in order until the assembly is apparently ready to close nominations.

    1. When there are two or more nominees for the office the motion to close nominations requires a two-thirds vote. (This motion must be seconded.) (See 4, opposite.)

    2. A negative vote on the motion to close nominations is an obvious criticism of the chairman for putting this motion to a vote too soon.

e. If the Chair recognizes a member and that member moves "that nominations close" (and it is seconded) before ample opportunity has been given for nominations from the floor, the Chair should ignore this premature motion by simply asking, **"Are there further nominations?"** instead of stating the motion "to close nominations." If and when there are no further nominations the Chair may then put the motion "to close nominations" to a vote without waiting for it to be moved a second time.

    1. The Chair is particularly responsible for protecting the rights of the minority. If the Chair participates in any scheme to "put something over on the assembly," the Chair is guilty of breach of trust. A chairman is presumed to be honest, fair, and politically intelligent.

1.   Elections (and nominations) must conform to the procedure (if there be any) prescribed by the Constitution and By-Laws.

2.   In case of a tie vote, the election is decided by lot unless the organization adopts a motion to do otherwise.

3.   Elections should be by ballot to reduce the personal friction of elections to the minimum.

4.   The motion "to close nominations and instruct the secretary to cast a ballot for the nominee" (or a "slate" of nominees) is in order **only** when there is **obviously** no opposition for the office or offices and when ample opportunity has been given for nominations from the floor.

    a.   This motion is a legal fiction by which an office is filled "by ballot" without an actual ballot vote by the members of the assembly.

    b.   This motion requires a unanimous vote.

Chairman:—"The 'Ayes' have it by unanimous vote. Nominations are closed, and the secretary is instructed to cast a ballot for the nominee. Mr. —— is declared elected to the office of ——. The next business is ——." (Consult secretary if in doubt.)

"No" vote:—(If any one votes in the negative) **"The 'Noes' have it and the motion to close nominations is lost. Are there any further nominations?"** (Presumably the opponents of this motion will make one or more additional nominations.)

5.   The motion "to suspend the rules and elect by acclamation" is in order **only** when the Constitution permits suspension of the election rules. Even when permitted by the Constitution, this procedure usually requires a two-thirds or a three-fourths vote.

6.   The motion "to make the vote unanimous" has no legal status, is not "carried" (adopted) if one member objects or votes "No," and can be moved **only** by the candidate next highest in the election just held.

20L.   TO RESCIND (or Repeal)

Member:—"Mr. Chairman" (Pause for recognition) "I move that we rescind (or repeal) the motion that (state motion to be rescinded)."

Chairman:—"It is moved and seconded that we rescind the motion that (state motion to be rescinded). Is there any discussion?"

Put to VOTE:—"The vote is on the motion to rescind the motion that (state the motion to be rescinded). Those in favor of the motion to rescind say 'Aye'. (Pause) Those opposed say 'No'."

"Aye" vote:—"The 'Ayes' have it, and the motion to rescind is carried. The motion to (state motion to be rescinded) is rescinded. Is there any other business?"

"No" vote:—"The 'Noes' have it and the motion to rescind is lost. Is there any other business?"

1	2	3	4
May apply to the following motions	May interrupt a member who has the floor	Mover must first be recognized	Requires a second
Main motions, appeals, questions of privilege	No	Yes	Yes

To Rescind or Repeal.

1. Is a "specific" main motion.

2. **Not in order when the subject can be reached by "reconsideration."**

3. Cannot be applied to action that cannot be reversed.

4. Requires two-thirds vote of members present, or majority vote of entire membership unless previous notice has been given of this particular motion to rescind.

5. Only majority vote of members present is required when notice of this particular motion to rescind was given at the previous meeting, or in the call for this meeting.

5	6	7	8
Debatable	Vote required	May be renewed	Motions that may apply to it
Yes	Majority (See 4 & 5)	Not at same session	All

To Amend the Rules

1. Is a main motion. (See chart for Main Question.)

2. Procedure is usually prescribed in Constitution or By-Laws.

3. Usual practice requires either two-thirds vote at one session or a majority vote in two successive sessions.

19L.

Member:—"Mr. Chairman" (Pause for recognition) "I move that we reconsider the vote on the motion (state the motion)."

Chairman:—**"It is moved and seconded that we reconsider the vote on the motion** (state the motion). **(If debatable) Is there any discussion on the motion to reconsider?"**

Put to VOTE:—**"The vote is on the motion to reconsider the vote on the motion** (state the motion to be reconsidered). **Those in favor of the motion to reconsider say 'Aye'.** (Pause) **Those opposed say 'No'."**

"Aye" vote:—**"The 'Ayes' have it, and the motion to reconsider is carried. You now have before you the motion to** (state the motion being reconsidered). **Is there any discussion on this motion?"** (If motion being reconsidered is not debatable, it is put to a vote without discussion.)

"No" vote:—**"The 'Noes' have it and the motion to reconsider is lost. The next business is** (consult secretary as to next business). **Or, is there any further business?"**

1	2	3	4
May apply to the following motions	May interrupt a member who has the floor	Mover must first be recognized	Requires a second
Any motion except adjourn, suspend rules, lay on table	Yes, for entry (See 3, 4, & 6)	No	Yes

Rules

1. Has high privilege for entry but not (necessarily) for consideration and vote.

2. May interrupt a member who is speaking (for entry, but not for consideration and vote).

3. Must be moved by one who voted with the prevailing side (unless vote was by ballot).

4. For actual consideration and voting its precedence is that of the motion to which it applies.

5. It suspends action on the motion to which it applies until it has been decided.

6. It is in order at the same meeting or during the next succeeding legislative day ONLY after the vote to which it applies was taken.

7. May be applied to all motions except to adjourn, to suspend the rules, or to table.

8. Requires only majority vote in all cases.

9. Has no privilege **for consideration** other than that of the motion to which it applies.

10. Not debatable if motion to which it applies was undebatable.

11. No question can be twice reconsidered.

12. Action that cannot be reversed cannot be reconsidered.

13. Can not reconsider negative vote on motion to postpone indefinitely.

14. Can not reconsider negative vote on a motion that may be renewed "after progress."

5	6	7	8
Debatable	Vote required	May be renewed	Motions that may apply to it
Yes (See 10)	Majority	No	Limit or close debate, lay on table, postpone definitely

18L.

Member:—"Mr. Chairman" (Pause for recognition) "I move that we," etc.

Chairman:—"It is moved and seconded that we (state the motion). Is there any discussion?"

Put To VOTE:—"The vote is on the motion that we (state the motion). Those in favor of the motion say 'Aye'. (Pause) Those opposed say 'No'."

"Aye" vote:—"The 'Ayes' have it, and the motion is carried. Is there any further business?" (Consult secretary.)

"No" vote:—"The 'Noes' have it and the motion is lost. Is there any further business?" (Consult secretary.)

1	2	3	4
May apply to the following motions	May interrupt a member who has the floor	Mover must first be recognized	Requires a second
No other motion	No	Yes	Yes

Substitute Motion

Member:—"Mr. Chairman" (Pause for recognition) "I move, as a substitute motion, that we (state the substitute motion)."

Chairman:—"It is moved and seconded as a substitute motion that we (state substitute motion). Is there any further discussion on the original motion, or on the substitute motion?"

(At this time either the original motion or the substitute motion or both may be perfected by detailed amendments.)

(When there is no amendment pending and no further discussion, the Chair should say)—

Put to VOTE:—"The vote is on the substitution of the last motion for the original motion. Those in favor of the substitution say 'Aye'. (Pause) Those opposed to the substitution say 'No'."

"Aye" vote and "No" vote (see other side at bottom of page).

Rules

1. Takes precedence of nothing and yields to everything except another principal motion offered later.
2. Should be in writing if complicated.
3. May be divided, if advisable, by motion to divide it.
4. Not in order if any other motion is pending.
5. When once decided, a particular main motion cannot be taken up again at that meeting.

5	6	7	8
Debatable	Vote required	May be renewed	Motions that may apply to it
Yes	Majority	Not at same session	All

Rules for Substitute Motion

1. A substitute motion is just an amendment that changes an entire sentence or paragraph.
2. It may be amended (like any other amendment).
3. It differs from an amendment only in that the motion to substitute, if adopted, does away entirely with the original motion.

"Aye" vote:—"**The 'Ayes' have it, and the last motion is substituted for the original motion. Is there further discussion on the motion that was substituted?**" (The vote is next on the adoption of the motion that was substituted, but the form is, of course, the same as though it were the original motion, or the motion as amended. Therefore, go next to **Put To VOTE** phrase above on opposite page.)

"No" vote:—"**The 'Noes' have it and the motion to substitute is lost. Is there any further discussion on the original motion (or the original motion as amended)?**"

17L.

Member:—"Mr. Chairman" (Pause for recognition) "I move that we postpone consideration of this motion indefinitely."

Chairman:—"It is moved and seconded that we postpone consideration of this question indefinitely. Is there any discussion on the motion to postpone indefinitely?"

Put to VOTE:—"The vote is on the motion that we postpone consideration of this question indefinitely. Those in favor of the motion to postpone indefinitely say 'Aye'. (Pause) Those opposed say 'No'."

"Aye" vote:—"The 'Ayes' have it, and the motion to postpone indefinitely is carried. Is there any other business?" (Consult secretary.)

"No" vote:—"The 'Noes' have it and the motion to postpone indefinitely is lost. Is there any further discussion on the main question that we (state pending motion)." (Go to page 18, left, **Put to VOTE** phrase next.)

1	2	3	4
May apply to the following motions	May interrupt a member who has the floor	Mover must first be recognized	Requires a second
Main motion, question of privilege	No	Yes	Yes

Parliamentary Strategy

Note:—When an important matter is unexpectedly brought before the assembly as a main motion it is of great value to the opposition to learn how many members are in favor of this main motion before the main motion comes to a vote. This is accomplished by the opposition moving to postpone indefinitely. This opens the main question to debate (see rule 2) and the opposition then gives their arguments against the main question. When the vote is finally taken on the motion to postpone indefinitely those opposed to the main question will vote for the motion to postpone indefinitely, while those in favor of the main question will vote against the motion to postpone indefinitely.

If the motion to postpone indefinitely is carried, the opposition to the main question are satisfied because the consideration of the question is

Rules

1. Takes precedence of only the main question.
2. Opens main question to debate.
3. Removes subject for the session.
4. Applies only to main question and questions of privilege.
5. Does not yield to amendments.
6. Not subject to subsidiary motions except "close debate."

Parliamentary Strategy:—The only purpose of the motion to postpone indefinitely is to enable the opposition to see how the assembly will vote on the main question without having the main question actually come to a vote. (See note below.)

5	6	7	8
Debatable	Vote required	May be renewed	Motions that may apply to it
Yes	Majority	No	Limit or close debate, reconsider ("I" vote only)

now indefinitely postponed and can not be brought before the assembly at this session, or at any time this month except by the motion to reconsider.

If the motion to postpone indefinitely is defeated, the Chair then asks for discussion on the main question at which time the opposition, seeing that they are outnumbered, can use this opportunity to obstruct to the limit or to compromise. The opposition, having learned the actual strength of those favoring the main question, are now in a position to do whatever they think best. In short, the only purpose of the motion to postpone indefinitely is to check a surprise attack. It is of use only to the opposition to the main question.

Member:—"Mr. Chairman" (Pause for recognition) "I move that we amend the motion by (adding, striking out, inserting) the words ——."

Chairman:—**"It is moved and seconded that we amend the motion by** (state the amendment), **so that the motion, if amended, will read that we** (state the motion as it would be changed by the amendment). **Is there any discussion on the amendment?"**

Put To VOTE:—"The vote is on the amendment that we (state the amendment). **Those in favor of the amendment say 'Aye'.** (Pause) **Those opposed say 'No'."**

"Aye" vote:—**"The 'Ayes' have it, and the amendment is carried. The next business is the motion as amended which reads that we** (state motion as amended). **Is there any discussion on the motion as amended?"** (Go to page 18, left, **Put To VOTE** phrase.)

"No" vote:—**"The 'Noes' have it and the amendment is lost. Is there any further discussion on the original motion?"** (Go to page 18, left, **Put to VOTE** phrase.)

1	2	3	4
May apply to the following motions	May interrupt a member who has the floor	Mover must first be recognized	Requires a second
Main motion, limit debate, refer, postpone definitely, fix time of next meeting	No	Yes	Yes

Amendment to the Amendment

Member:—"Mr. Chairman" (Pause for recognition) "I move that we amend the amendment by (adding, striking out, inserting, **substituting) the word ——."**

Chairman:—**"It is moved and seconded that we amend the amendment by** (state the amendment to the amendment), **so that the amendment, if amended, will read that we** (state the amendment as it would be changed by the amendment to the amendment). **Is there any discussion on the amendment to the amendment?"**

Put to VOTE (see other side at bottom of page).

Rules

1. Takes precedence of only the motion to which it applies.
2. May be amended (by "an amendment to an amendment").
3. May be divided (if incoherent) by motion to divide it, even after debate is closed.
4. Chair decides propriety of amendments, subject to appeal.
5. Chair may demand that amendments be in writing.
6. Neither yields to nor has precedence over motion to postpone indefinitely.
7. An amendment to an amendment cannot be amended. Amendments of the third degree are not permitted.
8. To table, postpone or refer an amendment to the main question is the same as tabling, postponing or referring the main question itself; consequently the motion to table, postpone or refer must be applied to the main question instead of to the amendment for the sake of clarity.

Form:—Amendments: "add, strike out, insert, strike out and insert, substitute or divide."

5	6	7	8
Debatable	Vote required	May be renewed	Motions that may apply to it
Yes	Majority	No	Amend, reconsider, limit or close debate

Amendment to the Amendment

Put to VOTE:—"The vote is on the amendment to the amendment that we (state the amendment to the amendment). Those in favor of the amendment to the amendment say 'Aye'. (Pause) Those opposed say 'No'."

"Aye" vote:—"The 'Ayes' have it, and the amendment to the amendment is carried. The next business is the amendment as amended which reads that we (state the amendment as amended). Is there any discussion on the amendment as amended?" (Go to Put to VOTE phrase above, opposite page.)

"No" vote:—"The 'Noes' have it and the amendment to the amendment is lost. Is there any further discussion on the original amendment?" (Go to Put to VOTE phrase above, opposite page.)

Member:—"Mr. Chairman" (Pause for recognition) "I move that
we refer this question (or resolution) to (state the committee
or person to which it is being referred)."

Chairman:—"It is moved and seconded that we refer this pending
motion (or motions) to (state the committee or person to
which it is being referred). Is there any discussion on the
motion to refer?"

Put To VOTE:—"The vote is on the motion to refer the
pending motion (or motions) to (state the
committee or person to which it is being referred). Those in
favor of the motion to refer say 'Aye'. (Pause) Those opposed
say 'No'."

"Aye" vote:—"The 'Ayes' have it, and the motion to refer is carried. Is there any other business?" (Consult secretary as to
next business.)

"No" vote:—"The 'Noes' have it and the motion to refer is lost.
Is there any further discussion on the pending question which
is (state the original motion or the amendment that is immediately pending)?"

1	2	3	4
May apply to the following motions	May interrupt a member who has the floor	Mover must first be recognized	Requires a second
Main motion, questions of privilege	No	Yes	Yes

To Amend the Motion to Refer

Member:—"Mr. Chairman" (Pause for recognition) "I move that
we amend the motion to refer by (adding the words) (state
the words to be changed)."

Chairman:—"It is moved and seconded that we amend the motion
to refer by (state the amendment) so that the motion to refer
if amended, will read that we (state the motion to refer as it
would be changed by the amendment). Is there any discussion on the amendment to the motion to refer?"

Put to VOTE:—"The vote is on the amendment to the motion to
refer which reads (state the amendment to the motion to
refer). Those in favor of the amendment to the motion to
refer say 'Aye'. (Pause) Those opposed say 'No'."

"Aye" vote and "No" vote (see other side, at bottom of page).

Rules

1. Debatable both as to instructions to the committee and as to the advisability of commitment.
2. May be amended by changing or instructing the committee.
3. Takes precedence over amendment to main motion, and over motion to postpone indefinitely.
4. Cannot be applied to subsidiary motions.
5. If no standing committee exists, the motion to refer should include the size of the committee and the method of selecting the members.

5	6	7	8
Debatable	Vote required	May be renewed	Motions that may apply to it
Yes (See 1)	Majority	After progress	Amend, reconsider, limit or close debate

"Aye" vote:—"The 'Ayes' have it, and the amendment to the motion to refer is carried. The next business is the motion to refer as amended which reads that we (state motion to refer as amended). Is there any discussion on the motion to refer as amended?" (Go next to **Put To VOTE** phrase above on opposite page.)

"No" vote:—"The 'Noes' have it and the amendment to the motion to refer is lost. Is there any discussion on the original motion to refer?" (Go next to **Put to VOTE** phrase above on opposite page.)

Member:—"Mr. Chairman" (Pause for recognition) "I move that we postpone consideration of this motion till the next meeting." (Or till the January meeting, etc.)

Chairman:—"It is moved and seconded that we postpone consideration of this motion till (state time to which postponed). Is there any discussion as to the advisability of postponement?"

Put To VOTE:—"The vote is on the motion to postpone consideration of the pending motion (or motions) till (state time to which postponed). Those in favor of the motion to postpone definitely say 'Aye'. (Pause) Those opposed say 'No'."

"Aye" vote:—"The 'Ayes' have it, and the motion to postpone definitely is carried. Is there any other business?" (Consult secretary as to next business.)

"No" vote:—"The 'Noes' have it and the motion to postpone definitely is lost. Is there any further discussion on the (original motion or the amendment, or whatever is immediately pending)?"

1	2	3	4
May apply to the following motions	May interrupt a member who has the floor	Mover must first be recognized	Requires a second
Main motion, questions of privilege, reconsider	No	Yes	Yes

To Amend Motion to Postpone Definitely

Member:—"Mr. Chairman" (Pause for recognition) "I move that we amend the motion to postpone definitely by (state the words to be changed)."

Chairman:—"It is moved and seconded that we amend the motion to postpone definitely by (state the amendment) so that the motion to postpone definitely, if amended, will read that we (state the motion to postpone definitely as it would be changed by the amendment). Is there any discussion on the amendment to the motion to postpone definitely?"

Put to VOTE:—"The vote is on the amendment to the motion to postpone definitely which reads (state the amendment). Those in favor of the amendment to the motion to postpone definitely say 'Aye'. (Pause) Those opposed say 'No'."

"Aye" vote and "No" vote (see other side, at bottom of page).

Rules

1. Applies only to the main motion.

2. Takes precedence of motion to refer, amend, or postpone indefinitely.

3. May be amended, but only by altering the time.

4. If the intent is to create a special order for the time fixed, this motion requires a two-thirds vote.

5. The motion postponed becomes a general order for the day named and cannot be taken up sooner except by two-thirds vote, unless the motion to reconsider is still in order.

6. Debatable **only** as to the propriety of postponement.

5	6	7	8
Debatable	Vote required	May be renewed	Motions that may apply to it
Yes (See 6)	Majority (See 4)	After progress	Amend, reconsider, limit or close debate

To Amend Motion to Postpone Definitely

"Aye" vote:—"The 'Ayes' have it, and the amendment to the motion to postpone definitely is carried. The next business is the motion to postpone definitely as amended, which reads that we (state motion to postpone definitely as amended). Is there any discussion as to the advisability of postponement?" (Go next to **Put to VOTE** phrase above on opposite page.)

"No" vote:—"The 'Noes' have it and the amendment to the motion to postpone definitely is lost. The next business is the original motion to postpone consideration till (state the time). Is there any discussion as to the advisability of postponement?" (Go next to **Put to VOTE** phrase above on opposite page.)

Member:—"Mr. Chairman" (Pause for recognition) "I move that we close debate and vote immediately on the pending question." (Note:—If there are several motions pending a member may "move to close debate and vote immediately on all pending questions.")

Chairman:—"It is moved and seconded that we close debate and vote immediately on the pending question. Those in favor of closing debate say 'Aye'. (Pause) Those opposed say 'No'."

"Aye" vote:—"The 'Ayes' have it by a two-thirds vote, and the motion to close debate is carried. The next business is the vote on the** (original motion or amendment or whatever it is), **which reads that we** (read the immediately pending motion). **Those in favor of the** (original motion, amendment, or whatever it is) say 'Aye'. Those opposed say 'No'."

"No" vote:—"The 'Noes' have it by more than a one-third vote and the motion to close debate is lost. Is there any further discussion on the** (original motion, amendment or whatever is immediately pending)?"

1	2	3	4
May apply to the following motions	May interrupt a member who has the floor	Mover must first be recognized	Requires a second
Any debatable motion	No	Yes	Yes

To Limit Debate

Member:—"Mr. Chairman" (Pause for recognition) "I move that debate be limited (to twenty minutes or to five minutes for each speaker or to three speakers on each side) or (that debate close at ten o'clock)."

Chairman:—"It is moved and seconded that debate be limited to (twenty minutes). Those in favor say 'Aye'. (Pause) Those opposed say 'No'."

"Aye" vote:—"The 'Ayes' have it by a two-thirds vote, and the motion to limit debate to** (twenty minutes) **is carried. Discussion is now on the** (original motion, amendment, or etc.)."

"No" vote:—"The 'Noes' have it by more than a one-third vote and the motion to limit debate is lost. Is there any discussion on the** (original motion, amendment or etc.)?"

Rules

("I move the Previous Question" is the old, brief way of moving to close debate.)

1. Takes precedence of all debatable questions and all subsidiary motions except "to lay on the table."

2. Requires a two-thirds vote.

3. Its effect is confined to the immediately pending motion be it subsidiary motion, amendment, or main motion unless it specifically indicates otherwise, as, "close debate on all pending questions, or all subsidiary motions, or all motions except the main question."

4. When ordered, no additional subsidiary motion may be introduced except "to lay on the table."

5. Cannot be debated nor amended.

6. Cannot have any subsidiary motion applied to it, nor to the main question while it is pending except the motion to lay on the table.

5	6	7	8
Debatable	Vote required	May be renewed	Motions that may apply to it
No	⅔ majority	After progress	Reconsider

To Limit Debate

1. Rules same as motion to close debate, except as to amendment.
2. May be amended.
3. Does not cut off other subsidiary motions.
4. Is debatable if made as a motion.

"Question!" "Question!"

When members of the assembly call out informally, "Question! Question!" it means only that they as individuals are ready to vote on the pending question or motion. It is their informal answer to the chairman's query, "Are you ready for the question?" This informal "call for the question" by members of the assembly must be clearly differentiated from the formal motion "to close debate and vote immediately on the pending question," or (what is exactly the same thing) the formal "I move the Previous Question."

Member:—"Mr. Chairman" (Pause for recognition) "I move that we table the main motion."

Chairman:—**"It is moved and seconded that we table the motion** (state the motion). **Those in favor of the motion to table say 'Aye'.** (Pause) **Those opposed say 'No'."**

"Aye" vote:—**"The 'Ayes' have it, and the motion** (state the motion) **is tabled. Is there any other business?"**

"No" vote:—**"The 'Noes' have it and the motion to table is lost. Is there any further discussion on the motion** (state the motion immediately pending) **?"**

1	2	3	4
May apply to the following motions	May interrupt a member who has the floor	Mover must first be recognized	Requires a second
Main question, appeals, questions of privilege, reconsideration	No	Yes	Yes

To Take From The Table

Member:—"Mr. Chairman" (Pause for recognition) "I move that we take from the table the motion to (state the motion that was **tabled).**

Chairman:—**"It is moved and seconded that we take from the table the motion to** (state motion that was tabled). **Those in favor of taking this motion from the table say 'Aye'.** (Pause) **Those opposed say 'No'."**

"Aye" vote:—**"The 'Ayes' have it, and the motion to take from the table is carried. You now have before you the motion to** (state motion taken from the table). **Is there any discussion on this motion?"** (Go to page 18, left, **Put To VOTE** phrase.)

"No" vote:—**"The 'Noes' have it and the motion to take from the table is lost. Is there any other business?"**

1	2	3	4
May apply to the following motions	May interrupt a member who has the floor	Mover must first be recognized	Requires a second
Only to motion that was "tabled"	No	Yes	Yes

Rules

1. Takes precedence of all other subsidiary motions.
2. May be applied to main motion, to appeals, to reconsideration, and to privileged motions that arise under questions of privilege.
3. Is in order when motion to close debate is pending or has been carried.
4. Cannot be debated or amended.
5. Not in order immediately after assembly has voted down objection to consideration.—(Has voted to consider the main motion.)   (See page 11–8.)
6. Cannot have any subsidiary motion applied to it.
7. Cannot apply to any subsidiary motion.

5	6	7	8
Debatable	Vote required	May be renewed	Motions that may apply to it
No	Majority	After progress	None

To Take From The Table

Rules

1. Has status of a "special" main motion.
2. Precedence is same as any main motion.
3. May be moved same day motion was tabled.
4. Cannot be moved when any other motion is before the assembly.
5. Is not debatable.   (But main motion will be debatable **if taken from the table.**)
6. No subsidiary motion may be applied to it.   (But any subsidiary motion may be applied to the main motion **if taken from the table.**)

5	6	7	8
Debatable	Vote required	May be renewed	Motions that may apply to it
No	Majority	After progress	None

table the undesirable motion in the first place?", since a bare majority can pass the motion to lay on the table and this subsidiary motion is undebatable. There are two reasons why the motion to lay on the table does not serve as well as the motion "objection to consideration" in disposing of very bad motions. The first reason is that a motion "laid on the table" may be "taken from the table" by a simple majority vote at any time after it has been "laid on the table." Consequently, a motion that is "tabled" may be only temporarily disposed of, whereas a motion "thrown out" by "objection to consideration" can not be brought before the assembly again at that session. The second reason is that the motion to "table" can not be moved when another member has the floor. Consequently, if some crank makes a motion, gets it seconded, and then starts to make a crazy or nasty speech on it, he can not be interrupted by the motion to "table," because the motion to "table" may not be moved when another member has the floor. But "objection to consideration" may be moved when another member has the floor; consequently, it may be used to stop a speaker right in the midst of his speech, provided two-thirds of the assembly are in favor of preventing "consideration of the motion." To repeat, objection to consideration is a motion that is not often used, but it is invaluable when needed.

PARLIAMENTARY STRATEGY
Strategic Use of the Motion to Postpone Indefinitely

The motion to postpone indefinitely is not a useful motion from the standpoint of its direct effect, because it is just as easy to vote down the main motion as it is to pass the motion to postpone indefinitely, since both are debatable and both have the lowest possible precedence. The real value of the motion to postpone indefinitely is strategic. It is the motion by which the opposition to a motion can ascertain the number of members for and against the main motion without the risk of having the main motion adopted.

If, at a national luncheon club convention, someone moves that the dues be increased ten dollars per member, those opposed to this increase in dues should move at once to postpone consideration of this motion indefinitely. Then they should present all their general arguments against the increase. When the vote is finally taken on the motion to postpone indefinitely, the opposition to the increase in dues are in the position of advantage. If the motion to postpone indefinitely is carried, the motion to increase the dues ten dollars is "thrown out" and can not be brought up again at that convention. On the other hand, if the motion to postpone indefinitely is defeated, the opponents of the raise in dues still have the advantage of having learned how large a majority are in favor of the increase, thus enabling them to determine just how many members now in favor of the increase must be won over to the opposition in order to defeat the main motion when it comes up for final vote.

In short, the motion to postpone indefinitely is the strategic motion used by the opposition to reveal the strength of the advocates of the main motion without the risk of having the main motion adopted. Having secured this information, the leaders of the opposition are better able to plan their political campaign against the final passage of the main motion.

OUT OF ORDER

One of the most difficult situations for a chairman is when a proposal, or person, or remark, is "out of order," because this involves an abrupt change in the orderly sequence of activities. In effect the chairman says, "Stop! you cannot do that." But the chairman himself may not stop at this point. He must go on to explain why it is "out of order," then tell the assembly what is "in order" at this point.

A **motion** is "out of order" when it is moved while a motion of higher precedence is pending. A **person** is "out of order" when he starts to make a speech without being recognized by the Chair, or when the person speaking is not a member of the club, and therefore has no "right to the floor." **Remarks** are "out of order" when they are insulting, profane, or otherwise offend the sense of decency of the club. Remarks are also "out of order" when they violate some rule of the club such as the rather common club rule that "neither partisan politics nor religious creeds may be discussed at club meetings."

The important point for the chairman to remember is that when some motion, or person, or remark is "out of order" the chairman must make three separate statements and make them promptly, as follows:—

1. The motion (or person, or remark) is "Out of Order."
2. Explain why it is "out of order." (At this point any two members may appeal from this decision. See Appeals, page 6.)
3. Tell the assembly what is now "in order," such as "Is there any further discussion on the motion to refer."

(Note:—For detailed instructions as to the duties of officers and committees, as to the conduct of committee meetings, especially committee of the whole, and as to the formulation and acceptance of committee reports, consult the larger treatises on parliamentary or legislative procedure.)

INFORMAL PROCEDURE
UNANIMOUS CONSENT—COURTESY VOTES

It is a mistake for a chairman to be unnecessarily formal. Matters of importance should, of course, be decided by a formal vote. But when there is obviously general approval on minor details these details should be handled informally by unanimous consent.

For example—

Mr. A:—"MR. CHAIRMAN."

Chairman:—"MR. A."

Mr. A:—"I MOVE THAT WE HAVE A SUPPER DANCE NEXT FRIDAY NIGHT."

Mr. B:—"I SECOND THE MOTION."

Chairman:—"It IS MOVED AND SECONDED THAT WE HAVE A SUPPER DANCE NEXT FRIDAY NIGHT. IS THERE ANY DISCUSSION?"

Mr. C:—"MR. CHAIRMAN."

Chairman:—"MR. C."

Mr. C:—"I AM ENTIRELY IN FAVOR OF THE PROPOSED DANCE. BUT I SUGGEST THAT THE WORD 'SUPPER' BE CHANGED TO THE WORD 'DINNER' BECAUSE IT IS CUSTOMARY TO CALL SUCH AN AFFAIR A 'DINNER DANCE' REGARDLESS OF HOW LATE THE DINNER MAY BE SCHEDULED."

Chairman:—"I BELIEVE YOU ARE CORRECT. DO YOU ACCEPT THAT CHANGE, MR. A?"

Mr. A:—"YES. I ACCEPT THAT CHANGE."

Chairman:—"THEN IF THERE IS NO OBJECTION THE WORD 'SUPPER' WILL BE CHANGED TO 'DINNER'. IS THERE FURTHER DISCUSSION ON THE MOTION TO HAVE A DINNER DANCE NEXT FRIDAY NIGHT?"

Mr. D:—"MR. CHAIRMAN, I RISE TO A QUESTION OF PRIVILEGE?"

Chairman:—"STATE YOUR QUESTION OF PRIVILEGE."

Mr. D:—"IT IS VERY WARM IN THIS ROOM. MAY WE HAVE THE WINDOWS OPENED A LITTLE?"

Chairman:—"IF THERE IS NO OBJECTION, THE SER-
GEANT AT ARMS WILL OPEN THE WINDOWS FOR
VENTILATION."

(Note. If some one does object then a formal vote is necessary
to determine whether the windows are, or are not, to be opened.
In very cold weather the persons near the windows may be just
as insistent on keeping the windows closed as others are on having them opened.)

Chairman:—(Continuing after windows are opened) "IS THERE
FURTHER DISCUSSION ON THE MOTION TO HAVE
A DINNER DANCE?" (*Pause.*) "IF NOT, THE VOTE IS
ON THE MOTION TO HAVE A DINNER DANCE.
THOSE IN FAVOR SAY 'AYE'." (*Pause.*) "THOSE
OPPOSED SAY 'NO'."

A Courtesy Vote

There is one situation in which the negative vote is not called
for; that is where the vote is merely an act of courtesy. For instance, when a guest speaker has given an address it is common
practice for some member to move that the speaker be given a
rising vote of thanks.

The chairman says, "IT IS MOVED AND SECONDED
THAT WE GIVE OUR GUEST SPEAKER A RISING VOTE
OF THANKS. THOSE IN FAVOR PLEASE RISE." (*Pause.
The members rise and frequently applaud also.*)

In this case the negative vote is not called for because, after
all, nothing is being decided that binds the organization in any
way. Nevertheless, a few negative votes would be quite a discour-
tesy to the guest speaker and would embarrass him considerably.

However, both the chairman and the members should see to
it that these courtesy votes are not used as an endorsement of
the cause which the speaker presented in his speech or as an endorsement of the speaker personally for some office for which
he is a candidate.

Nothing short of intelligence, watchfulness, and loyalty to
the group will suffice to keep a given group from being used by
ambitious persons to further their own selfish ends. An intelli-
gent, alert chairman can easily prevent any member from thus
violating the rules and purposes of the organization by refusing
to put an improper motion to a vote or by calling the attention of
the group to the danger involved in the motion presented to them
for a vote.

But when the chairman is disloyal to the aims and purposes
of the group, it is not so easy for loyal members to keep improper
motions from coming before the assembly for consideration and
vote. Therefore, when a chairman persists in attempts to divert

the group from its established rules and purposes, it is both proper and wise for the loyal members to move "that the chairman be censored for ignoring the rules and purposes of the organization."

Of course, the quickest way to deal with an improper motion moved by any member and stated by the Chair, is to "rise to a point of order" and then state that the motion before the assembly is improper because it violates the rules or purposes of the group. And if the Chair decides that "your point is not well taken," you can appeal from the Chair's decision to the assembly. (*See appeals, page 6 in manual. Also see lesson XIII in Senior Manual for Group Leadership.*)

If two-thirds of the group are opposed to the consideration of the motion in question it can be "thrown out" just as soon as it is moved by the use of "objection to consideration." (*See page 11 in the manual. Also see lesson XIII in Senior Manual for Group Leadership.*)

NOMINATIONS

One outstanding duty of the citizen is to help choose the leaders of his group. This is done by means of nominations and elections. In small groups nominations are usually made "from the floor," that is, a member rises and addresses the Chair. When recognized by the Chair the member says, "I nominate Mr. John H. Smith for president." A nomination by this method does not require a second, but other members may desire to "second" this nomination just to show that they support Mr. J. H. Smith for this office. When there are no other nominations to be made some member should move, "that nominations close." If this motion is seconded and adopted by a two-thirds vote, nominations are closed and the group may then proceed with the final election.

Another form of nomination is to have a nominating committee make up a list of one or more nominees for each elective office and present these nominations to the group in the form of a committee report. Frequently this form of nomination is supplemented by "nominations from the floor." A nominating committee has the advantage that it can consult each nominee in advance and be sure that the nominee will accept the nomination when it is made. Also, a nominating committee can make up "a slate" of nominees for the various offices who will work together harmoniously if all the members of this "slate" are elected. It is a misfortune for any group to have a chairman and a secretary who do not cooperate cordially in conducting the affairs of the group.

A third method of nomination for an elective office is to have a certain number of members (one or more) sign a petition placing Mr. J. H. Smith in nomination for the office of president. This method is too slow and cumbersome except for a very large group.

A PRACTICE NOMINATION

Chairman: "THE MEETING WILL COME TO ORDER. THE FIRST ITEM OF BUSINESS TODAY IS THE NOMINATION OF CANDIDATES FOR THE ANNUAL ELECTION TO BE HELD AT THE NEXT REGULAR MEETING. ALL NOMINATIONS ARE TO BE MADE FROM THE FLOOR. NOMINATIONS FOR THE OFFICE OF PRESIDENT ARE NOW IN ORDER."

Mr. A:—"MR. CHAIRMAN."

Chairman:—"MR. A."

Mr. A:—"I NOMINATE JOHN BLACK."

Chairman:—"JOHN BLACK IS NOMINATED."

Mr. B:—"MR. CHAIRMAN."

Chairman:—"MR. B."

Mr. B:—"I NOMINATE MARY BROWN."

Chairman:—"MARY BROWN IS NOMINATED."

Miss C:—"MR. CHAIRMAN."

Chairman:—"MISS C."

Miss C:—"I SECOND THE NOMINATION OF MARY BROWN."

Mr. D:—"MR. CHAIRMAN."

Chairman:—"MR. D."

Mr. D:—"I SECOND THE NOMINATION OF MARY BROWN."

Chairman:—"ARE THERE FURTHER NOMINATIONS?"

Miss E:—"MR. CHAIRMAN."

Chairman:—"MISS E."

Miss E:—"I NOMINATE WALTER JONES."

Chairman:—"WALTER JONES IS NOMINATED."

Miss C:—"MR. CHAIRMAN."

Chairman:—"MISS C."

Miss C:—"I NOMINATE CHARLES BRADFORD."

Chairman:—"MISS C HAS ALREADY SECONDED THE NOMINATION OF ONE CANDIDATE AND THERE-FORE CANNOT NOMINATE ANOTHER CANDIDATE. IN SOME STATES THERE IS A LAW AGAINST SIGN-ING THE PETITION OF MORE THAN ONE CANDI-DATE FOR THE SAME OFFICE."

Mr. F:—"MR. CHAIRMAN."

Chairman:—"MR. F."

Mr. F:—"I NOMINATE CHARLES BRADFORD."

Chairman:—"CHARLES BRADFORD IS NOMINATED."

Mr. A:—"MR. CHAIRMAN."

Chairman:—"MR. A."

Mr. A:—"I MOVE THAT NOMINATIONS CLOSE."

Mr. F:—(*without waiting for recognition*) "I SECOND THAT MOTION."

Chairman:—(*momentarily ignoring that motion*) "ARE THERE OTHER NOMINATIONS?" (*After a pause in which no further nominations are made.*) "IF NOT, IT IS MOVED AND SECONDED THAT NOMINATIONS BE CLOSED. THOSE IN FAVOR OF CLOSING NOMINATIONS SAY 'AYE'." (*Pause*) "THOSE OPPOSED SAY 'NO'."

Chairman:—"THE 'AYES' HAVE IT BY A TWO-THIRDS VOTE, AND THE MOTION TO CLOSE NOMINATIONS FOR THE OFFICE OF PRESIDENT IS CARRIED. NOMINATIONS ARE NOW IN ORDER FOR THE OFFICE OF VICE-PRESIDENT."

Note: Nominations may be reopened by a simple majority vote when there is occasion for doing so.

NOMINATION BY NOMINATING COMMITTEE

Chairman:—"THE MEETING WILL COME TO ORDER. THE FIRST ITEM OF BUSINESS TODAY IS THE REPORT OF THE NOMINATING COMMITTEE. AT THE LAST MEETING MOLLIE BLACK, CHESTER BRADLEY, AND FRANK OAKLEY WERE SELECTED AS THE NOMINATING COMMITTEE. IS THE NOMINATING COMMITTEE READY TO REPORT?"

Mollie Black:—"MR. CHAIRMAN."

Chairman:—"MISS BLACK."

Mollie Black:—"IN ACCORDANCE WITH THE PROVISIONS OF THE CONSTITUTION YOUR NOMINATING COMMITTEE DESIRES TO PLACE IN NOMINATION THE FOLLOWING PERSONS:
FOR PRESIDENT, MARY BROWN; FOR VICE-PRESIDENT, CHESTER WINSLOW; FOR SECRETARY, VIRGINIA BRADFORD; FOR TREASURER, FRANK LUDLOW; FOR SERGEANT AT ARMS, FRED BRITTON."

Chairman:—"YOU HAVE HEARD THE REPORT OF THE NOMINATING COMMITTEE. OUR CONSTITUTION ALSO PROVIDES FOR NOMINATIONS FROM THE FLOOR. ARE THERE OTHER NOMINATIONS FOR PRESIDENT? (*Pause. Hearing no nominations, he continues*) FOR VICE-PRESIDENT? (*Pause, hearing none*) TREASURER? (*Pause, hearing none*) FOR SERGEANT AT ARMS?"

Chairman:—"IF THERE ARE NO OTHER NOMINATIONS WILL SOMEONE PLEASE MOVE THAT NOMINATIONS BE CLOSED AND THAT THE SECRETARY BE INSTRUCTED TO CAST A BALLOT FOR THE 'SLATE' OF NOMINEES PRESENTED BY THE NOMINATING COMMITTEE."

Note:—This suggestion by the chairman that someone move that the secretary be instructed to cast a ballot for the nominees would be out of order at this meeting if the Constitution provided that nominations be made at one meeting and the election be held at the next meeting. Even a unanimous vote can not suspend the Constitution unless the Constitution specifically provides for such suspension (which it usually does not).

Chester Bradley:—"I MOVE THAT NOMINATIONS CLOSE AND THAT THE SECRETARY BE INSTRUCTED TO CAST A BALLOT FOR THE 'SLATE' OF NOMINEES."

Frank Oakley:—*(without waiting to be recognized)* "I SECOND THE MOTION."

Chairman:—"IT IS MOVED AND SECONDED THAT NOMINATIONS CLOSE AND THAT THE SECRETARY BE INSTRUCTED TO CAST A BALLOT FOR THE 'SLATE' OF NOMINEES PRESENTED BY OUR NOMINATING COMMITTEE. THOSE IN FAVOR OF THIS MOTION SAY 'AYE'." *(Pause. Many vote "Aye.")* "THOSE OPPOSED SAY 'NO'." *(None vote "No.")*

Chairman:—"THE 'AYES' HAVE IT UNANIMOUSLY, AND THE MOTION IS CARRIED. THE SECRETARY WILL CAST A BALLOT FOR EACH OF THE NOMINEES. IS THERE ANY OTHER BUSINESS?"

Note:—In case someone votes "No" on the above motion, the motion is lost because it requires a unanimous vote. When this motion is lost because of one or more negative votes, the chairman may ask those voting in the negative to make other nominations since they seem to be opposed to the present nominees. But whether other nominations are made or not, a separate vote must be taken for each office to be filled when the motion "to instruct the secretary to cast a ballot" has been defeated by one or more negative votes.

As a matter of fact, formal nominations are not necessary for an election. The members may proceed to "ballot" on the election of a "president" for instance, and each member may write on his ballot the name of the person he desires for president. Then the ballots are counted and all the names written on the ballots are listed as candidates with the number of ballots received by each candidate listed after the name of that candidate If only a plurality vote is required for election the candidate with the largest vote on the first ballot is declared elected. If a majority vote is required for election then some rule must be followed for the succeeding balloting that will insure a majority vote for some one candidate after a reasonable number of votes have been taken. The usual rule in such cases is to drop the candidate with the smallest vote after each balloting until a majority vote is secured. Sometimes the rule is adopted that after the first ballot all but the two candidates with the highest votes are dropped. This simple rule guarantees a majority vote at the end of two ballotings. However, this system offers clever politicians an easy opportunity to eliminate good candidates on the first ballot by nominating other candidates who will "split-the-vote" of the good candidates so that the two candidates who survive the first ballot may not be the two strongest candidates in the list of original nominees.

Note:—The best method of preventing this political trickery is by using the single-transferable-vote system described in the section below on Elections.

ELECTIONS

When the candidates for an elective office have been nominated, the next step is to elect one of the nominees for the office to be filled. For this purpose two general systems are used, majority election and plurality election. In a plurality election the candidate having the largest number of votes is declared elected even though this candidate actually received only twenty-five per cent of the total vote. In fact, if there are ten nominees, one of them may be elected under this system by a vote of twelve per cent if each of the other nine candidates receives close to ten per cent of the total vote.

However, the majority vote system is considered the better system because it guarantees that the leader elected represents the choice of a majority of the members. There is no system of choosing leaders that will *guarantee* successful leadership, but obviously a leader with a majority supporting him at the beginning of his term of office has a better chance to be a real leader of the group than a leader with the support of only twenty per cent of the membership at the beginning of his term of office.

There are two systems of choosing officers by majority vote: one is the system of double elections, that is, a primary election to reduce the number of candidates to two, and a final election to choose between these two. This is the system in most common use in the United States. The other system is called the "single-transferable-vote system" because you mark your first, second, third and perhaps a fourth choice on the ballot and then your second choice vote is counted if your first choice candidate runs lowest in the count of the first choice votes. This system does away with two elections but it does take a little more time to count the ballots.

Under this single-transferable-vote system all the first choice votes are counted and placed in piles, one pile for each candidate. Then, if no candidate gets a majority of the total vote, the candidate having the smallest first choice vote is declared "out of the race" and his first choice ballots are all re-counted in accordance with the second choice indicated on each ballot. If the addition of these second choice ballots does not give any candidate a majority of the total vote, the candidate with the lowest total on this second count is declared out of the race and his ballots are re-counted according to the next choice on each ballot. This system of dropping off the lowest candidate continues either until one candidate does get a majority of the total vote, or, failing in that, until there is only one candidate remaining. Usually, one candidate will eventually secure a majority under this system if the voters will indicate their second, third and fourth choices as well as their first choice. Voters should mark a second, third and fourth choice under this system, because the second choice is not a vote against the first choice owing to the fact that the second choice is not counted until the first choice is declared "out of the race."

In principle this single-transferable-vote system is the same as the double election system because in a primary election you vote your first choice and then, when your first choice candidate is eliminated in the primary, you go to the voting booth at the final election and vote your second choice. Under the single-transferable-vote system you indicate both your first and second choice at the one election so that when your first choice candidate turns out to be the "tail end" candidate, the election officials can go ahead and count your vote for your second choice because you have already indicated your second choice on the one and only ballot.

No illustration is necessary to explain the ordinary primary and secondary (or final) election. One ballot is taken and if no one gets a majority of all the votes cast, all but the two leading candidates are dropped from the contest and then a second vote is taken on the two remaining candidates.

The other majority vote system (the single-transferable-vote system) requires some illustration to make it clear. The voter indicates his first, second, third and fourth choice by the numbers 1, 2, 3 and 4. The voter marking the ballot to the right voted for Mary Brown as his first choice, Walter Jones as his second choice and John Black as his third choice.

Ballot	Choice
John Black	3
Mary Brown	1
Walter Jones	2
Charles Bradford	

He refused to give Charles Bradford his fourth choice because he did not want Charles Bradford as president under any circumstance.

When the ballots for this class of thirty members were counted according to the first choice votes the count was as indicated in the first count column below.

Candidate	1st Count 1st Choice only	Jones' Ballots 2nd Choice	2nd Count 1st & 2nd Choice	Bradford's Ballots 2nd Choice	3rd Count
John Black	8	1	9	2	11
Mary Brown	10	3	13	5	18
Walter Jones	4	—	—	—	—
Charles Bradford	8	0	8	—	—
Exhausted Ballots	—	—	—	1	1
Total Ballots	30	4	30	8	30

The first choice ballots are arranged in piles by the "tellers" with all of the eight John Black 1st choice ballots in one pile, all of the ten Mary Brown 1st choice ballots in another pile, etc.

Since no candidate has a majority of all the votes cast the candidate with the smallest vote, Walter Jones, is declared "out of the race" and his four 1st choice ballots are re-distributed according to their 2nd choice indication. (See 2nd column above.) Adding these 1st and 2nd choices together gives the second count which is 9, 13 and 8 respectively for the three remaining candidates. Still no candidate has a majority of all the votes cast, consequently, the candidate with the smallest vote in this 2nd count, Charles Bradford, must be dropped and his eight 1st choice ballots re-distributed according to their 2nd choice indication which is shown in column 4. One of the Charles Bradford 1st choice ballots had no 2nd choice indicated, therefore it was an "exhausted ballot" when Bradford was declared "out of the race." These 2nd choice ballots for John Black and Mary Brown are added to their previous total of 9 and 13 respectively to make the 3rd count of 11 for John Black and 18 for Mary Brown. Mary Brown now has 18 ballots which is 2 more than a majority of the total vote cast, therefore, Mary Brown is declared elected to the office of president for the next year.

By this system a group can select its officers by majority vote with one brief election no matter how many candidates are nominated. The counting of the ballots may take some time, but this need not delay the group as a whole. Three "tellers" can take the ballots to another room and do the counting (if desirable, under the supervision of the candidates or their representatives) while the group as a whole adjourns, or proceeds to take up other business.

Committees are usually appointed by the Chair. But where it is preferred that the members of a committee be elected, several methods of election are available. If it is a committee of five, each member may vote for any five candidates and the five candidates with the largest vote are declared elected. (This is called straight election-at-large.) This method has the disadvantage that a bare majority of fifty-five per cent of the members may elect all the members of this committee, leaving the forty-five per cent minority of the club membership without any representation on this important committee.

A simple system that guarantees some representation for a strong minority is that known as limited voting. If a committee of five is to be elected, each voter is allowed only one vote (instead of five as above). Under this system it will usually work out that the fifty-five per cent majority will elect three members of the committee while the forty-five per cent minority will elect two members.

The most accurate system of choosing a committee or a board of directors that accurately represents each group in the club in proportion to its numerical strength is known as the "Hare System of Proportional Representation," but this system is too complicated to be explained here. (See description of this system in the Encyclopedia Brittanica.) The ballot is the same as that used to elect a president by the single-transferable-vote system described above, but the counting of the ballots is much more complicated.

When there is a tie vote for two candidates, the tie is usually broken by flipping a coin. Since half the group favor each candidate, it does not matter much which one is finally chosen, consequently, deciding it by chance is the simplest solution of the problem.

SECRETARY AND MINUTES

The secretary (or clerk) of an organization is the next officer in importance to the chairman because he (or she) keeps the official record of the action of the organization. However, there are many organizations in which the secretary is the officer of most importance. This is when the secretary is the one who knows all the past history and precedents of the organization and tells the chairman just how things have been done in the past and should be done in the future. In these instances the chairman may change every year, but the secretary is re-elected (or re-hired) year after year.

In addition to keeping accurate minutes of each meeting, the secretary must have a thorough knowledge of parliamentary procedure, must be able to read papers and communications to the assembly with a clear voice, and must be able to preside in the absence of the chairman and vice-chairman.

Since the secretaryship is primarily a working job rather than an honorary one, the secretary should be chosen because of his (or her) accuracy, speed in taking notes, and knowledge of procedure rather than because of popularity. The business of the organization is soon in chaos if the secretary is unable to present the old business and the new business in proper order or fails to keep accurate minutes of the various meetings.

The final report of the minutes, sometimes called "The Journal," should be typed or written legibly in ink, never in pencil. The minutes should tell the kind of meeting (regular or special), the date of the meeting, the name of the organization and the name of the presiding officer. The minutes should contain a record of all the formal actions of the organization and this should be certified by the signature of the secretary. When these minutes are approved at the next meeting this action should be recorded at the bottom of the minutes as follows:—

"Approved as read (or approved as corrected) May 26, 1955."

_____

Signature of Secretary.

Since the secretary should not slow up the business of the meeting by taking time to write out every action in full, some rapid system of note-taking should be used. The following is offered as one good system of note-taking.

MATERIALS FOR NOTE-TAKING

The secretary should have on hand a good pen and plenty of ink, or not less than two pencils well sharpened. For paper, a loose-leaf notebook is best if the pages are securely fastened. Loose sheets of paper may be blown from the table by an unexpected gust of wind, making it necessary to delay the business of the meeting while the secretary collects the scattered papers from the floor.

The minutes of the previous meeting should be immediately to the left, (in front) of the blank pages to be used for recording the business of the current meeting. This makes it easy to refer to the past action of the organization when there is occasion for doing so.

MINUTES — O — BLANK PAGES

To facilitate the business of a meeting the secretary should make a list of the old business at the top of the blank page to be used in recording the notes of this meeting. For example:—

OLD BUSINESS FOR MEETING OF NOV. 2, 1955.
  To have a picnic—Tabled Oct. 26.
  To have a dance—Postponed (Oct. 26) to Nov. 2.
  To raise dues—Referred to Finance Com. for report at Nov. 2 meeting.
  To buy a radio—Pending at adjournment. (Unfinished Business.)

"Old business" includes motions referred to committees, motions postponed to later meetings and motions tabled, as well as "unfinished business" which is the motion (if any) that was pending when the last meeting was adjourned. The motions referred to committee may come back before the assembly as committee reports. The motions postponed till a later meeting come before the assembly again as general orders or special orders. The motions laid on the table may be brought before the assembly again by the motion "to take from the table." (See bottom of page 12 in manual.) The motion that was pending at the time of adjournment of the last meeting (and is, therefore, unfinished business) comes up automatically at the next meeting at the time specified in the "Order of Business" for unfinished business.

GENERAL AND SPECIAL ORDERS

An "order" is something which a majority (perhaps an extraordinary majority) of the assembly has commanded. If a majority of the assembly orders that the motion to have a radio be considered at the November second meeting, then this motion to have a radio has precedence at the November second meeting over a motion that is sponsored by only two members of the assembly such as a new motion to have a Christmas Party.

Obviously the majority of the assembly should have the authority, when they desire it, to say what motions are to be considered at the next meeting and in what order. The command (by the motion to postpone) that a certain matter be considered at the next meeting is called a "general order." The command that a certain matter be considered at a certain definite time ("at 3 o'clock" or "immediately after the reading of the minutes") is called a "special order." To create a special order requires a two-thirds vote. (See pages 8 and 14 in manual.) And a special order can not be changed except by a two-thirds vote. Usually general and special orders are created by means of the motion "to postpone to a certain day" (see page 14 in manual). However, these orders may be created by a main motion. For example, when there is no other business before the assembly a member may rise and say, "Mr. Chairman." The chairman recognizes him:—"Mr. Smith." Mr. Smith says, "I understand that Judge Parmelee is to speak to us at the next meeting. Judge Parmelee is an able and distinguished speaker. It will be a great privilege to hear him. Since he is a very busy man, I believe we should make his talk the special order for that day so that he may address us just as soon as he arrives no matter what other business may be pending at that time." If this motion is seconded and carried by a two-thirds vote, then Judge Parmelee's talk is the special order for the next meeting and the chairman is ordered to present him to the assembly just as soon as he arrives regardless of what other business is pending at that time.

General or special orders may be created by the Constitution or By-Laws. Thus many Constitutions (or By-Laws) provide that "the annual election of officers shall be held the first meeting in September" (a general order). Or "the election of officers for the new year shall be held immediately after the reading of the minutes at the September meeting" (a special order). Such an order being a "constitutional order" can be changed, of course, only by suspending or amending the Constitution. "Orders," whether general, special or constitutional, are called "Orders of the Day" for the meeting to which they apply.

The secretary should have a list of the orders of the day, if there be any, ready for the chairman to use in announcing to the assembly the order of business for that meeting. If the chairman fails to present to the assembly some item of business that is an order of the day for that meeting, a member may remind him by rising and without waiting to be recognized calling out, "Mr. Chairman, I call for the orders of the day!" (See page 4 in manual.)

Committees that are to report at this meeting should be listed on the memorandum sheet much the same as special and general orders so that none will be forgotten.

XL

Committee Reports
    Social Committee—Year's Program
    Finance Committee—Budget

Abbreviations, symbols and diagrams are of great value in recording events quickly. For instance: "Have picnic. J. Brown" is all that is necessary to record that "J. Brown moved that the Lincoln Athletic Club give a nice picnic somewhere. This was seconded." If the secretary has already written down a motion which was declared out of order or lost for want of a second this should be noted as follows:—

Have picnic—J. Brown. { lost, no second, or, out of order.

Plenty of space should be left below each main motion so that all subsidiary, incidental and privileged motions moved may be shown in their proper relation to this main motion. The following will illustrate:—

Have picnic—J. Brown.
    at Sunset Park
    Lay on Table (better still, just "Table").

or Have dance—H. Smith.
        at Trilby Hall
       at 8:30 Saturday night
        Refer to Social Com,
        Close Debate
    Table

Adjourn

The motion to adjourn is not attached to the main motion because it does not apply to the main motion. It applies to the assembly. The motion to close debate is attached to the motion to refer because it applied to debate on the motion to refer and not to debate on the amendment or on the main motion. The motions to table, to refer and both amendments are attached to the main motion, because each of these subsidiary motions did apply to the main motion. When in doubt as to what motion may be applied to what other motion the secretary may find out instantly by looking at item one or item eight in the chart under each motion in the manual.

When the main motion has been disposed of in some manner so that there is no pending motion before the assembly it is worthwhile to make this clear by marking a line clear across the page like this :—

Have a dance—H. Smith.   Carried.
      ⌐at Trilby Hall Friday night. Carried.
           ⌐Close debate.   Carried.

Have a card party—
       ⌐Friday night, Nov. 14.
      ⌐Refer to Social Com.   Carried.

The illustration below will show how a more complete record may be kept with the minimum of writing by the use of the diagram together with a reference letter for each motion and the addition of two words to the action taken.

```
a.... Have a dance—J. Brown........carried after c.
b....        ┌ at Trilby Hall......carried when moved.
c....        at 8:30 Sat. night......carried after h.
d....     refer to Soc. Com.   ......lost after e.
e....        close debate      ......carried after f.
f....        Table             ......lost
g....     Adjourn              ......lost
h....     close debate all     ......carried after d.
```

The order in which the motions come in the diagram shows the order in which they were moved. In case a motion applies to a motion not immediately above it, this may be indicated by connecting it directly to the motion to which it applies with a half circle to show where this connecting line crosses the line of motions to which it does not apply. If more than one motion is pending when the motion to close debate on all pending questions is carried, this motion to close debate should be attached to the motion immediately pending. The word "all" after the motion to close debate makes it clear that it does apply to all pending questions.

FINAL MINUTES OF MEETING OF JAN. 10, 1955

The regular monthly meeting of the Lincoln Athletic Club was called to order by the President, John Tremain, Monday, January 10, 1955 at 2:00 o'clock in the gymnasium. The minutes of the previous meeting were read and approved. A motion by J. Brown to raise the dues from 25 to 50 cents a month beginning with the month of March, 1955 was carried. A motion by H. Smith for the Athletic Committee to arrange with Garfield School for a track meet was also carried. The motion by Mary Jenkins to donate $25 to the school charity fund was tabled. A motion by Harry Jones to have a dance was postponed till the next meeting. The report of the Social Committee on the Year's Activity Calendar was unanimously accepted. The treasurer's report for the year 1954 was received and placed on file (see footnote below). Having no further business the meeting was adjourned.

Mary Jane Brown,

Secretary.

John Tremain,

    President.

Footnote:—The treasurer's report should not be accepted until it has been carefully examined by an auditing committee and checked against the receipts, cancelled checks, cash on hand, etc. The treasurer's report is "received and placed on file" for the auditing committee. The report of the auditing committee is "accepted" or "rejected."

Note:—A very good collection of model minutes, committee reports and other forms used by organizations will be found in the appendix to "Textbook on Parliamentary Law" by Hall and Sturgis, published by Macmillan, 1930.

NOTES FOR MEETING FEB. 7, 1955.

Preliminary Memorandum for Chairman

1. Call meeting to order.

2. Reading and approval of Minutes.

3. Orders of Day,
   a. Special Orders,
      None.
   b. General Orders,
      Have dance—Postponed from Jan. 10.

4. Unfinished Business—None.

5. Committee Reports.
   a. Athletic Com.—On Garfield Sch. track meet.
      Finance Com.—On Budget for 1955.

6. New Business,
   In order here "to take from table motion to donate $25.00 to School Charity Fund" tabled Jan. 10.

1. Called to order by Jack Tremain, Pres. 2:15 P. M.

2. Minutes approved as corrected.
   Correction—Motion to raise dues moved by Fred Johnson instead of J. Brown.

3. a.... Have a dance ....Carried after e.
   b.... at Trilby Hall ....Carried after c.
   c.... Refer to Soc. Com. ....Lost after d.
   d.... Close Debate ....Carried
   e.... March 19, at 8:30 ....Carried after f.
   f.... Table ....Lost.

4. None.

5. Athletic Com. Report
   Lincoln-Garfield Track Meet July 1, approved.
   Finance Com. Report.
   Proposed Budget for 1955 referred back to Com.

6. a.... Take from table.... Carried.
   b.... Donate $25.00 to School Charity Fund. Cd. after e.
   c.... in weekly payments of $5.00 Cd. after d.
   d.... close debate Cd.
   e.... beginning March 1 Cd. after c.

---

a.... Have orchestra.   John Graham.   Lost after f.
b.... Postp. to next meeting   Lost after d.
c.... Ref. to Music   Com. Out of order, b pending.
d.... Close debate   Lost after e.
e.... Table   Lost.
f .... Adjourn   Lost after b.

---

a.——Moved—Audit committee of three be appointed by Chair to audit Treasurer's accounts. Mary Powers. Carried after b.

b.—— Strike out 3, insert 5   Lost.

Chair appointed Harvey Benson, Mary Powers and Fred Goldman.

Adjourn—Carried 3:10 P. M.

M. J. B.

XLIV

The regular monthly meeting of the Lincoln Athletic Club was called to order by the President, John Tremain, Monday, Feb. 7 at 2:15 in the gymnasium. The minutes of the previous meeting were read and approved as corrected.

The motion to have a dance, postponed at the January meeting, was carried after being amended to read that we have a dance at Trilby Hall March 19 at 8:30.

The Athletic Committee reported that arrangements had been made with Garfield School for a Track Meet July first. This was approved.

The Finance Committee presented the budget for the year 1955. This was referred back to the committee for further consideration.

The motion to donate $25.00 to the school Charity Fund was taken from the table and carried after being amended to read that we donate $25.00 to the school Charity Fund in weekly payments of $5.00 beginning March 1.

A motion to have an orchestra was moved by John Graham, seconded and lost.

It was moved by Mary Powers, seconded and carried that an Audit Committee of three be appointed by the Chair to audit the treasurer's accounts. The Chair appointed Harvey Benson, Mary Powers, and Fred Goldman for this committee.

The meeting adjourned on motion at 3:10 P. M.

Mary Jane Brown,

Secretary.

John Tremain,

President.

DUTIES OF A SECRETARY

1. To keep a careful and authentic record of the proceedings of the organization.

2. To prepare a roll call of members and call it when necessary.

3. To call the meeting to order in the absence of the presiding officer.

4. To preserve all documents of the organization except those specifically assigned to others.

5. To provide the chairman of each committee with a list of

the members of his committee together with all the papers and instructions intended for it.

6. To provide the presiding officer at the beginning of each meeting with the order of business for that day.

7. To read all the papers that may be called for by the assembly.

8. To authenticate by his signature all records, documents, etc.

9. To bring to each meeting a copy of the constitution, by-laws, and the standing rules of the organization, together with a list of the members of all standing and special committees.

10. To carry on all official correspondence for the organization.

    a. When this duty involves much work it is frequently assigned to a correspondence secretary.

This manual and these lessons are designed to cover only the minimum essentials of parliamentary procedure. For a more complete discussion of motions, duties of officers, committees and committee reports consult the standard texts such as Robert's "Rules of Order," the "House Rules and Manual" (Congressional Manual), "Legislative Procedure" by Robert Luce, etc.